GW00394011

The Story of Corfe Castle

Seal of Corfe Castle

For Edward and Rome

The Story of
CORFE CASTLE

Edited by
EMMELINE HARDY

DOVECOTE PRESS

First published in 1983
This revised paperback edition
first published in 1988 by The Dovecote Press Ltd
Stanbridge, Wimborne, Dorset BH21 4JD

ISBN 0 946159 50 5

© Emmeline Hardy 1983, 1988

Cover illustration Paul Bale

Printed and bound by Biddles Ltd
Guildford and King's Lynn

5 7 9 8 6 4

My dear grandson,

You were four years old when you looked up at Corfe Castle from where we were standing by the stream. You remember, don't you? There was part of the castle in the stream, and you wondered how it got there, and if it made a big noise when it fell.

"Is there a book, Granny," you asked, "a book about the first Edward?"

I said I would try to find one.

Sometimes strange things happen, and something very strange happened about the book. I didn't find one right away, and as you know, Grannies are pretty busy people, so I had to look—just now and then—when I had a chance to do so.

About two months ago a friend came to stay. She had brought for me a gift from her daughter, "because they thought it would interest me." And, would you believe it? That book was the story of Corfe Castle! Neither of these friends knew I had wanted to find such a book.

It is a very old book, written nearly 150 years ago. The way of writing is charming, and the history very interesting. It is rather "grown up" for you at present. But I know you are going up into kindergarten next term and will soon be able to read things for yourself. What I have done is "to edit", which means "to alter" this book, making it easier for you.

For the time being I will tell you the stories from the book. Later on you can read them for yourself.

Then, if you still want to know more about the castle, you will learn how to find out about it in the historical records.

This new and edited story of Corfe Castle is for you, who at so early an age wanted to know more about your namesake "the first Edward", who was called the Martyr.

with love,

Granny

Danes in Swanage Bay

INTRODUCTION

This book, which I have edited and abridged, was originally published in 1853 by John Murray of London under the title *The Story of Corfe Castle, and many who have lived there.* The rather lengthy title page went on to add that the Story had been 'collected from ancient chronicles and records; also from the private memoirs of a family resident there in the time of the Civil Wars: which include various particulars of the Court of Charles the First, when held at York and afterwards at Oxford'. It's author may be forgiven his long-windedness, for he was the Right Honourable George Bankes, M.P. for Dorset and, more importantly, owner of Corfe Castle and a direct heir of the heroic Lady Mary Bankes.

My own copy was given to me, and the pleasing quaintness of the style of writing, the wealth of detailed information, and charming illustrations, have encouraged me to condense and edit the book for 'my Edward' mentioned on the previous page; who at the age of nine is constantly asking to be told about Corfe Castle and the 'first Edward'.

Corfe Castle's story is as remarkable as any. Murder, intrigue, romance, and a famous siege weave their way through its history. I have tried to make it more than a guide book, something that the many visitors who scramble over its ruins will want to keep as a memento of their ramble through the village and castle as they are today.

Emmeline Hardy
Swanage, 1988

PART ONE SAXONS
Saxons 871-1013

CHAPTER I

There is reason for concluding that a castle existed at Corfe in the reign of King Alfred.

Alfred was founder of the Abbey at Shaftesbury. To his daughter Ethelgiva, and to her successors, high rights and privileges were granted connected with Corfe Castle and the surrounding domain.

In his time the castle at Corfe consisted, probably, of only a single strong tower on the summit of the hill, constituting one of the defences against the depredations of the Danish and other pagan nations; and guarding Wareham, in those days a very important town and port.

In the year 875, four years after Alfred became king, he made an agreement with Hubba the Dane, and a partition, assigning to them a large portion of the northern provinces of his kingdom. Then, believing himself to be happy in the preservation of this kingdom, and anticipating a peaceful life, he looked forward to some leisure.

But he had misread the situation—considering the attacks by Danes as a regular war occupying the whole of the invading nation's armies. In fact this was not so, for the Danes proceeded on a totally different principle. Their king entered into private agreements to man fleets to attack and pillage England, going shares in the booty therefrom. Each band of invaders was a separate unit,

A.D. 871
King Alfred's
reign began

Corfe Castle
probably
Saxon Hall
typical of
that period

A.D. 875
Division of
Kingdom

*Division of
Alfred's
Kingdom*

13

independent of the others, and bound by no treaty unless entered into by themselves.

Alfred had made his agreement with Hubba; but in the spring of 875, Halfden, a Danish general, with a very considerable force, took by surprise Wareham Castle—then the strongest place in all Wessex. Halfden did not consider himself bound by the treaty made with Hubba. The English regarded the surprise attack on Wareham as a real treachery, and violation of the treaty. Alfred, finding it in vain to conclude treaties with such perfidious people resolved to take more effectual action.

Convening a General Assembly, he called on them to trust in their valour and courage to deliver them from their Danish master; not only venturing their lives, but to sacrifice part of their estates to preserve the rest, and to make a stand in defence of their country.

So an army was levied, with which he engaged the enemy seven times in one campaign. Fortune was not equally favourable to him in all these engagements, but he succeeded in making the town so little comfortable to the Danish overlords, that in 877 their army quitted Wareham, partly on horseback, and partly by water.

A.D. 877
Naval
Engagement
off Swanage
120 ships
destroyed
off Peveril
Point

The naval portion proceeded no farther than Swanage. There, attacked by ships provided by Alfred, and hindered by a furious storm coming on during the engagement, 120 of their ships were driven on the rocks off Peveril Point. All were destroyed.

The other portion of the army was pursued by Alfred as far as Exeter. Weakened as they were, they readily acceded to Alfred's terms, giving hostages, and departing the kingdom.

To effect security against their return in the future, was the object of a fortress at Corfe—

then called "Corffe's Gate"—a break in the lofty range of the Purbeck Hills occurring at this place, through which two small streams, the Wicken and the Byle, pursued their course to the not far distant sea.

In Alfred's time there were scarcely any but timber houses. It was he who induced the English to build houses for the future in a stronger and more regular manner than before. He raised his own palaces with stone or brick, and by degrees the nobility began to follow his example. Alfred encouraged noted workmen and architects, keeping them about him, constantly employed, improving their skills.

In the century following King Alfred, under the direction of King Edgar, who began his reign in the year 958, Corfe's castle was greatly extended and embellished. Italian workmen were brought to England to instruct and aid native artisans, accounting for some of the peculiarities of the structure, and the perfection of its masonry.

**A.D. 958
King Edgar's
reign began**

During his reign, Edgar the Peaceable, as he was called, raised the Anglo-Saxon dynasty to a high degree of renown, obtaining for himself the title of the Honour and Delight of the English Nation. He was so well prepared for war that neither his own subjects, nor other nations dared to disturb the tranquillity of his dominions. His attention to maritime affairs was the chief glory of his reign, and his fleet was at once so powerful and so well conducted, that it effectually secured the coasts from all aggression.

He retained also a permanent military force, composed of Danes; nor does it appear that any jealousy arose from this circumstance amongst the masses of his Anglo-Saxon subjects.

King Alfred

15

Anglo-Saxon homes

We are told by the ancient chronicles, that these martial Danes introduced such courtly fashions as the habit of combing their hair once a day, washing themselves once a week, and frequently changing their vestments—manners which, though censured as effeminate by the Anglo-Saxon nobles, met with the decided approval of their wives and daughters, the gay beauties of King Edgar's Court.

It was Edgar's queen who played such an important and terrible part in the history of Corfe Castle.

Edgar the Peaceable died in the thirty-third year of his age, bequeathing the castle to Elfrida as a dowry mansion. In this princely residence, which her royal husband had prepared for her with so much cost and care, she plotted and accomplished the murder of his son.

A.D. 975 Edward's reign began. Later known as "The Martyr"

Edward, the son of Edgar's first marriage, was only fifteen years of age when his father died. His stepmother, Queen Elfrida, vainly endeavoured to oppose his succession to the throne, in favour of her own son.

Edward ruled for four years, and was greatly beloved by his subjects, having earned their affection by the amiable innocence of his manners. As his own intentions were pure, he was incapable of entertaining any suspicion against others. Thus, though his stepmother had opposed his succession, and had raised a party in favour of her own son, he always showed her the greatest regard, expressing always the most tender affection towards his brother.

A.D. 978 Death of Edward at site of West Bailey

It was in March of the year 978 when this unfortunate prince was hunting in a large wood near Wareham. Towards evening, when the chase was ended, recollecting that his

16

brother was living hard by, he resolved to visit him at the castle, where he resided with his royal mother. The attendants of the king had been dispersed in the chase, and he was alone.

Elfrida having notice of this favourable opportunity to put her wicked plan into action, came forth in a most affable and friendly manner, inviting him to alight from his horse. He declined, remaining at the castle gate expressing his desire to see his brother.

The queen then called for some wine to refresh him. Scarcely had he put the wine to his lips, when one of her attendants, who had given the king the kiss of peace, stabbed him in the back. Some ancient chroniclers affirm that Elfrida herself gave him both the kiss and the mortal wound whilst he was drinking. Wounded, the king rode away, fainting with loss of blood. His foot entangled in the stirrup, and he was dragged a considerable distance before his horse stopped of its own accord at a bridge which crosses the small river that flows at the foot of the hill on which this castle stands. The queen sent a servant to learn the result of her treachery, and the murdered prince was found dead, terribly defaced with the flints over which he had been dragged.

Anglo-Saxon lady

*It was because of the manner of his death that the young king was remembered in history by the custom which first took rise at that time among the Anglo-Saxons, when they pledged each other: the person who was going to drink asked any one of the company that sat next to him, whether he would pledge him. On which, he answering that he would, held up his knife or sword to guard him whilst he

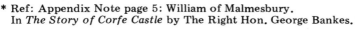

* Ref: Appendix Note page 5: William of Malmesbury.
In *The Story of Corfe Castle* by The Right Hon. George Bankes.

drank. (While a man is drinking he necessarily is in an unguarded posture, exposed to the treacherous stroke of some hidden or secret enemy.)

To conceal her wicked deed Elfrida ordered Edward's body to be lodged in a cottage nearby, where it was covered with such mean clothes as were at hand. The woman living in the cottage was born blind, and was maintained by the queen's alms. It is told that at midnight she found her sight restored, and to her great terror the house filled with light.

In the morning the queen was informed of this story, and became very frightened, and fearful of the discovery of her treachery. She ordered her attendants to throw Edward's body into a well, and then she fled to a mansion of hers called Bere, about ten miles distant.

Elfrida's own son Ethelred, hearing the story, expressed sorrow for the inhuman act of his mother. Because of this she beat him so severely with some heavy wax tapers, for want of something else at hand, that he hated the sight of them ever afterward!

Juvenile readers in particular may have some curiosity on this subject, and wish to be informed what sort of wax candles these were. A drawing-room candle could hardly inflict such a blow, as to induce the subject of correction to remember it during the whole remainder of his life. And a Chapel Candle, even the daring spirit of Elfrida would not have ventured to apply to such a purpose.

No, we must remember that one of the noble institutions of King Alfred being then, and long afterwards, in force, the lapse of time was measured by the gradual consumption of wax candles, and Elfrida, in fact, corrected

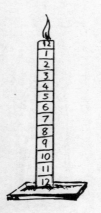

The castle clock may have looked like this!

18

her son with the castle clock! A weapon of no small weight and magnitude.

Alfred (we are told by the learned Spelman) measured time by means of wax candles marked by circular lines of divers colours, which served as so many hour lines. These candles were committed by him to the keepers of his chapel, whose office it was to put him in mind how each hour passed.

Glass was then a great rarity in England, so that the king, for the defending of these lights, was obliged to have recourse to white horn scraped very thin. Thus it was that Alfred became inventor at once both of clocks and lanterns.

Thin horn to protect from draughts

A year passed. The body of the murdered king was found; according to the record a pillar of fire descended from above illuminating the place where it was hid. Some devout people of Wareham brought the body of the king to the Church of St. Mary in that town, and buried it in a plain manner. From this time the place where the body had lain yielded pure and sweet water, being called St. Edward's Fountain, and infirm people were daily healed there.

News of these happenings being circulated, Alfer, Earl of Mercia, a faithful adherent of the deceased king, resolved to remove the body to a more suitable place of sepulture. Inviting all bishops, abbots, and nobility to assist him, he sent to Wolfrida, Abbess of Wilton, to come with her nuns and perform the funeral rites with due solemnity. The noble company thus convened, being joined by a great number of the country people, came to Wareham, where the body, on being taken out of the tomb in which it had lain three years, was found as free from corruption as on the day it was placed

19

there. It was carried on a bier to Shaftesbury. Among the concourse of people were two lame persons, who were cured on approaching the bier.

Elfrida, struck with remorse, prepared to join this noble funeral procession, hoping thus to make some atonement for her crime. But her utmost efforts could not prevent the horse she rode from running backwards. She tried several horses, being an intrepid lady; but not one of them would advance a step. She then attempted to go on foot, but with no better success.

The royal corpse was received at Shaftesbury by the abbess, and entombed at the north part of the principal altar. The manner of Edward's death, and the affection of the monks, whom he had much favoured, gained him the surname of Martyr. He was canonized by the Church of Rome, three festivals in every year being appointed to be kept as holy in respect of his memory— March 18th the day of his murder; February 18th, and June 20th, the days on which the removal of his corpse had been effected.

In consequence of the assassination of young Edward, the crown of England devolved on Ethelred, his half-brother, who was barely seven years of age. Aspiring to be his governor and the regent of his kingdom was Elfrida, blasted in character and powerless from loss of reputation.

In order to expiate the murder of Edward, and other crimes of which she was conscious, Elfrida had recourse to the general remedy of that age for an uneasy conscience, founding and endowing richly two nunneries. One at Amesbury in Wiltshire, the other at Whorwel in Hampshire. It was in Whorwel she took the

Habit, and spent the remaining years of her life in great penitence, austerity, and superstitious dread.

Then ensued a period which is justly considered as the most calamitous in English history. The piratical Danes, who for more than half a century had given the English little disturbance, began again to cast their rapacious eye on this country.

Ethelred, as he grew to manhood proved to be cowardly and sluggish. He seemed to have no predominant corrupt passion in his nature, but he lived in a time when activity and bravery were essential to the people who owned his sway. His surname of "The Unready" was proved apt. When he designed to oppose the landing of the Danes, they were in the heart of a county before he had brought his forces to the coast. When he resorted to the fatal plan of promising large bribes for their departure, he found, on the day fixed for payment that he was unprovided with the money. The rage and ravages of the invaders broke out with redoubled fury. Houses, monasteries, and churches built with timber were now destroyed by fire throughout all the the south-western counties.

A.D. 979
Ethelred's
reign began

A.D. 1013
Retired on
Sweyn's
Proclamation

Corfe Castle could set at defiance every attempt of the Danish force. But, with the exception of a few such places so fortified, all parts of Dorsetshire fell under the Danish rule.

The year was 1002. The whole kingdom stood in such fear of the Danish power, that the appellation of Lord Danes was given to them throughout the land. In that year the disgraceful tribute of Danegeld was fixed upon the nation. Ethelred found his subjects much irritated by the indignity of the tax, and of their slavish position, and willing to concur

21

Archer

with him in the infamous project of a general massacre of all the Danes then resident in England.

With wonderful secrecy of preparation this was carried into effect in one day. The slaughter included the sister of Sweyn the Dane. She was married to an English noble.

In the next year, thirsting for revenge, Sweyn, landing in Cornwall, marched to Exeter and entirely destroyed that city, putting all the inhabitants to the sword.

No misfortune which can befall a nation was now spared to the English. There was a grievous famine in 1005. For a brief spell the Danes returned to their native country—but with the first appearance of returning prosperity in England, they came again to resume their lordly demands.

**A.D. 1013-14
Sweyn's
reign began**

In 1014 Sweyn was acknowledged King of England, and Ethelred fled with his family to Normandy.

PART TWO DANES
*Danes 1013-1042
Restoration of Saxons 1042-1066
1066 Norman Conquest 1066-1154*

Sweyn died in the year he was made king—some thought by poison.

**A.D. 1014-16
Ethelred
reigned again**

With some difficulty Ethelred was induced to return to his own kingdom. After two more years of misery and contest, his ignoble reign ended, and brave Edmund, his eldest son, was immediately crowned in London.

22

But the curse of bloodshed seemed to rest upon his house. He reigned for less than a year—murdered by a traitor, one of his family, before the close of the year 1017.

A.D. 1017
Ethelred
murdered
(known
thereafter
as "The
Unready")

Edmund had two sons. Neither succeeded to the throne, and the line of his descendants excluded by the Danes—and afterwards by the Normans, was not restored to the crown until after the lapse of 600 years.

Corfe Castle, which from the time of the Norman Conquest was held as a royal castle by some great baron of the victorious race, followed the fortunes of the English crown during the various revolutions following upon the suppression of the Anglo-Saxon dynasty.

A.D. 1090
(approx)
Norman
Castle built
on site of
Saxon Hall

Henry I was crowned king in 1100, reigning for 35 years when he died at the age of 67. His only son was drowned, and the nobles had promised him that his daughter, Matilda, would reign at his death. Stephen disputed her claim, and it became at once evident that a serious civil war would ensue, and that the string of castles throughout the kingdom would exercise a great influence in deciding the issue of the quarrel. The beginning of his reign was peaceable, but this tranquillity lasted not long.

A.D. 1100
The Keep
known to
have been
standing at
this date

A.D. 1135
Stephen's
reign began

Many of those subjects whose affection Stephen had tried to gain by conferring titles and honours on several persons, and alienated abundance of the crown lands to such as might be serviceable to him, by now had grown insolent, setting too high a value on the service they had done the king. Others who received no favours entertained a jealousy which proved most injurious to his cause.

And there were some also who, being forced to comply with the majority, were waiting an opportunity to fulfil the oath given in favour of Matilda the daughter of the late king.

Stephen's greatest oversight was suffering the barons and the wealthy clergy to fortify their castles, which put it in their power to revolt whenever they pleased. Bishops, earls and barons at this time coined their own money in their castles. They exercised therein every right of sovereignty, extending to complete despotism.

A.D. 1139
Corfe Castle
held by
Baron de
Redvers at
this time

Stephen finally found himself under the necessity of besieging some of the castles. He took the castle at Devizes; forced Wareham to surrender; but was baffled in an attack upon Corfe Castle. It was a fortress of such strength, that until the invention of gunpowder, it could be taken by no other means than by treachery of the garrison.

The Civil War had raged so long and so violently that the strength of both parties was almost exhausted. A contemporary historian wrote:

'All England wore a face of misery and desolation. Multitudes abandoned their beloved country, and went into voluntary exile; others forsaking their own houses, built wretched huts in the churchyards, hoping for protection from the sacredness of the place; whole families, after sustaining life as long as they could by eating herbs, roots, and the flesh of dogs and horses, at last died of hunger; and you might see many pleasant villages without a single inhabitant of either sex.'

24

At last in the year 1153 these fearful national calamities were brought to a close by the Treaty of Peace, under which it was stipulated that Stephen should continue to reign during his life.

A.D. 1153 Treaty of Peace

Prince Henry, son of Matilda, should be his successor. A primary condition of this treaty was that all the castles built on both sides since the death of Henry I (amounting, it is said, to the number of eleven hundred and fifteen!) should be demolished.

This condition did not affect Corfe Castle, which had stood out against the power of Stephen the usurper, and proudly acknowledged the authority of Henry Plantagenet when, after the death of Stephen in the year 1154, without opposition he was called to the throne and crowned Henry II.

A.D. 1154 Death of Stephen and Henry II's reign began

PART THREE
Plantagenets 1154-1397

Corfe became a royal residence again in the eventful reign of the tyrannical John, who came to the throne in the year 1199.

A.D. 1199 John began to reign

John deposited within the castle walls his treasure and regalia. He used it also for the confinement of state prisoners, the objects of his jealousy and revenge.

In the year 1202, he took prisoners at the castle of Mirabel in Poitou, among whom was the youthful Prince Arthur, Duke of Brittany, his own nephew. At the same time he captured many barons, and above 200 hundred knights of Poitou and Guienne, who were at arms with that prince. Loaded with irons, they were sent to different prisons in Normandy and England. Many were so cruelly treated that they

A.D. 1201-04 Fortification of West Bailey and three towers built

25

perished in their confinement. No fewer than twenty-two of the noblest and bravest of them were starved to death in Corfe Castle.

Prince Arthur was murdered at the instigation, or perhaps by the hand of his cruel uncle.

A.D. 1202 Forfeiture of all Continental Lands held by John

The barons of Brittany accused John of this crime before the King of France, of whom John held all his continental territories. When he did not appear to answer to that charge, he was found guilty of treason and felony, and all his dominions forfeited. He made little or no resistance at that time, abandoning the continent and embarking for England.

A.D. 1205 John professes attempted recovery of territories

In 1205 King John feigned with a resolution to attempt the recovery of his foreign territories, summoning all his barons and other military tenants to meet him at Portsmouth on Whit-Sunday. After much delay and frivolous conduct, he at last embarked with a small retinue, and put to sea. For two days he continued out of sight of land, then returned, landing at Studland, and proceeding to Corfe Castle. Here he made

A.D. 1207 Great Ditch was dug between Keep and Outer Bailey

proclamation to the effect that he had been on a foreign expedition; fined all his military tenants for their non-attendance, and thus added a further accumulation to his ill-gotten treasure.

A.D. 1212 Prophecy

Now there was a hermit, one Peter of Pomfret, who had foretold that the king in this very year should lose his crown. For that rash prophecy he had been thrown into prison in Corfe Castle.

A.D. 1213 King John's treachery

In the year 1213, on 15th May, King John resigned England, and Ireland, to God, to St. Peter, and St. Paul, and to Pope Innocent and his successors, doing homage to Pendolf, as the Pope's Legate, with all the humiliating

26

forms which the feudal law required from vassals towards their liege lord and superior.

Eventually, owing to the insistent demands of the barons, on 19th June, 1215, King John unwillingly signed the Magna Carta. This charter laid down what the barons recognised to be fundamental principles for the government of the realm. It bound king and barons alike to maintain them. It stated among other things, that no man should be punished without fair trial, and that ancient liberties generally should be preserved.

Immediately the Magna Carta was granted by King John he became sullen, melancholy and dejected. He retired with a very few of his courtiers to the Isle of Wight, forming schemes for the recovery of prerogatives which he had relinquished. With this in view he dispatched orders to the commanders of all the royal castles to repair their fortifications, and furnish them with provisions.

The year which followed was the last of his wretched life. He was now in perpetual motion, not knowing whither to go, nor whom to trust. Carefully avoiding fighting, he incessantly marched from place to place. He thought himself safest in Norfolk, where he chose the town of Lynn to secure his treasures, including his crown and sceptre. This town had expressed for him such affection and loyalty, that as a mark of his gratitude he granted it great privileges, presenting to the first mayor his own sword. Then, fearing his treasures were not safe even here, his favourite town, he resolved to remove them into Lincolnshire. Endeavouring to effect this removal, he very narrowly escaped drowning with his whole army, in the Marsh, or Wash,

The miserable King John

27

which parts the two counties of Lincoln and Norfolk. He had himself barely effected the crossing, together with a portion of his forces, when the tide, coming rapidly up the river Well-stream, the Marsh was overflowed, and his baggage containing the treasure, also the remainder of his troops and attendants, were swallowed up by the waters.

He arrived that night at Swineshead Abbey, where he lodged. His vexation for this loss threw him into a violent fever, which he aggravated by eating largely of peaches. On the morrow he was carried on a litter to Seaford Castle, and thence next day to Newark. Some will have it that he was poisoned by a monk of Swineshead Abbey. But the stories of his being poisoned are various in their particulars. One attributes the king's death to the poison extracted from a toad put into a cup of wine; the other to a dish of poisoned pears, of which the monk who presented them ate three, which were not poisoned, leaving all the rest for the use of the king. But contemporary historians have not attributed his end to such a cause, nor is it asserted by anyone who wrote within sixty years of that time.

A.D. 1216 Death of King John

John was 50 years of age, and the year 1216. His unhappy reign had lasted for 17 years.

At the time of the death of King John, the Earl of Pembroke was Mareschal of England, who had always remained loyal to the previous monarch (Richard I). A man eminently wise, brave, and honest.

The whole land was torn by civil discord, and a large portion actually in the hands of a foreign power. The country required the energies of such a man.

28

The Earl of Pembroke assembled the lords who had been firm to the royal cause, and, presenting to them Prince Henry, then in the tenth year of his age, exclaimed: "Behold our King." This assembly then unaminously chose the Earl of Pembroke guardian of the king, and declared him Protector of the Kingdom. The earl immediately provided for the coronation of the prince, by the title of Henry the Third. This ceremony was performed in the city of Gloucester.

A.D. 1216
Henry III
crowned

A portion of the regalia was still at Corfe Castle. Being left there, it had escaped the fate of the remainder of King John's treasure.

The new protector demanded of Peter de Maulay, Constable of the Castle, that he deliver these for the king's use at the coronation. The crown here found was a plain circle or chaplet of gold, probably a Saxon crown.

At a later period of his reign Henry had a second coronation, in Westminster Abbey.

Corfe Castle was now delivered to the Earl of Pembroke, the Protector. An escutcheon, on one of the towers, bore his armorial device.

Found prisoner in this castle, where she had passed many sad years in the custody of her tyrant uncle, was the Princess Eleanora, called the Maid of Brittany. Within these walls also were found, besides jewels and other articles of value, large stores of military engines, which John had provided for the purpose of enforcing the subjugation of the barons, and the revocation of Magna Carta.

The French had been called in to take part in the intestine commotions of the state. The protector succeeding in effecting their expulsion, and by the prudence and equity of his conduct he reconciled the contending

A.D. 1216
Death of
the Protector

29

factions. He had adopted measures for recovering and securing possession of all the royal castles, but unhappily for the kingdom he died in the first year of the new reign.

Never was there a greater loss than that of this brave and good man. Lamentation was universal through the realm, and his memory revered and equally cherished by the various hostile parties who met in fierce contention through the remainder of this long and turbulent reign. To the young King Henry III this loss was irreparable.

We may recollect now that, when William the Conqueror claimed the land as his own in the year 1066, he divided it up as he pleased. When he wanted money he extorted it from the people.

Now, 200 years later, Henry III needed money for his wars.

Simon de
Montfort,
Earl of
Leicester
1206-65

But at this time arose a leader of the people, one Simon de Montfort, who feared nothing, and was prepared to do battle with the king. Again and again during this long reign, the king made promises and agreements, only to break them. The fighting continued, until at length Simon de Montfort succeeded in forming a Parliament which superseded the old Assembly of the Wise Men. Knights, bishops and barons from each county, and even citizens from the towns, had the right to come to say what the people in their part of the country wished to be done.

In a final battle at Lewes in Sussex, giving victory to Simon, Henry III was taken prisoner.

About nine years after the death of the protector, in defiance of the king, possession of Corfe Castle was resumed forcibly by Peter de Mauley, in the interest of Simon de

Montfort and his followers.

In such high consideration was Corfe Castle held by Simon de Montfort and the powerful barons who adhered to him, that it was the third which they demanded to be ceded to them when they exacted royal castles as pledges for the future good conduct of the king.

Hume, speaking of the character of Henry III, says that the most obvious circumstance was his incapacity for government. This rendered him as much a prisoner in the hands of his own ministers and favourites, as when detained a captive in the hands of his enemies.

During the reign of Edward II which commenced in 1307, it appears that Corfe Castle was put into a state of complete repair at the expense of the crown. Whether the king enjoyed this place of residence as a palace we are not informed; but it became his prison. By command of Queen Isabella, mother of the king, and Mortimer her paramour, Edward was taken out of the honourable custody of Henry Earl of Lancaster, his cousin, and confided to the keeping of two brutal men: Sir John Maltravers and Sir John Gournay (blemishes of knighthood as the old chronicles call them).

A.D. 1307 Edward II began to reign

A.D. 1326 14th Nov.

These two ungracious villains, with their attendants, had commission at any time to enter into any castle or fortress within the kingdom, and there to abide during their pleasure, commanding all within the place.

By them, therefore, he was removed from Kenilworth Castle in Warwickshire, where he had passed the previous winter, and hurried about in the night from one place to another, that no one might know certainly of his abode.

31

First, they brought him with all secrecy imaginable to the Castle of Corfe in Dorsetshire; thence awhile after to Bristol Castle, where they kept him privately in hardship and fear enough, till, it being scented by some of the chief citizens, out of a due commiseration of his undeserved troubles, and a just sense of the duty they owed him, they secretly combined to deliver him from these inhuman keepers, and so to convey him to some place of safety beyond the seas.

But his hard destiny permitted this counsel to take wind, insomuch that on the very night when his deliverance was to be effected, these, his inhuman keepers, removed him from Bristol and conveyed him to Berkeley Castle in Gloucestershire.

And here they showed the baseness and barbarity of their minds, making him ride on an ill-favoured beast; very meanly clad, who of late was lord of a great kingdom; and still they took by-ways crossing the country lest he should be met by any and rescued.

Nor did the insolent indignities they put upon him end there; for having a mind by and by to cut off the hair of his head and his beard, that he might be more disguised from the knowledge of any they should chance to meet, they made him alight at a certain ditch in their way, whence an insolent barber fetched them cold and dirty water in an old rusty helmet, as he sat on a molehill to be trimmed, the king meekly saying: "Whether you allow it or no, I will have warm water for my beard," and therewith let fall a shower of warm tears.

This story was attested by William Bishop, one of the accomplices, who was present at the doing thereof, and afterwards heartily repented that ever he had a hand in so wicked a concern.

And thus, at last, they brought him to Berkeley Castle, where, finding that poison would not affect his body, nor mental torture conclude his life, they, with barbarous violence destroyed him, pretending that he died a natural death. His body was exposed to public view, and wise men could not but observe by the colour of his face that his death was not without many violent struggles.

He was buried without any funeral pomp by the Benedictine monks, in their Abbey of St. Peter, in Gloucester.*

A.D. 1327
Death of
Edward II

During the reign of King Edward III, Corfe Castle was the scene of an extraordinary happening.

A.D. 1327
Edward III's
reign began

The Earl of Kent, brother to Edward II, had no great genius for public affairs. He was naturally a sincere and generous man. He had suffered himself to be deceived by Queen Isabella, joining with her against his own brother. Too late he saw the imminence of revolution.

The disorderly behaviours of the queen, the insolence of Mortimer, and the general ill-conduct of public affairs brought on him the realisation of her deceptions, and a deep repentance for the course he had taken. His open nature caused him to make his feeling

* Throughout the long reign of Edward III the particulars relating to the death of his father were variously related. In a history printed in the first volume of Harleian Miscellany, the murder of Edward II is stated to have been effected at the Castle of Corfe; of which castle it is further affirmed that this royal victim had a peculiar dread, derived from ancient predictions, which were, perhaps, founded on traditions relating to the fate of his martyred namesake.

known, and Isabella and Mortimer then resolved on his destruction. To this end they prepared for him a most extraordinary snare.

There had been rumours rife throughout the kingdom to the effect that Edward II was not dead. They used this rumour to further their plan.

Two persons, pretended friends, came to the Earl of Kent, and informed him that his brother, Edward II was still prisoner in Corfe Castle, strictly guarded, and suffered to be seen by none but his domestics, who were guarded with him. This pretended secret was confirmed by the testimony of several persons of distinction, including two bishops.

The earl himself had assisted at the private funeral of the king, his brother, but he had not seen the body. He feared he had been deceived, and to discover if this might be the case, determined to release him, if he were still alive.

Meanwhile, Queen Isabella (who, says Stow, "bore an inveterate hatred against Edmund Plantagenet, Earl of Kent"), began earnestly to inform the king her son against him, as guilty of matters into which the subtle Mortimer had craftily ensnared the earl.

And so Mortimer and his co-plotters cunningly scattered it abroad that the old king Edward II was still alive, and resided in the Castle of Corfe in Dorsetshire.

To carry on this incredible tale the better, there were several knights appointed to make shows and masks and other diversions upon the battlements and roofs of the castle, which the country people observing could not but imagine some great prince or king to be there, for whose pleasure and honour they were so performed.

So the rumour of the old king being alive
was spread far and near, so that at last it
came, as was at first designed, to the Earl of
Kent's ears, with some authority.

Desiring only, as he thought, to sift the
truth out, he entangled himself more strongly
in error.

To the Castle of Corfe he privily sent one
of his confidants, a preaching friar, with a
charge to dive into the matter. He at last, with
a great to do, obtaining to be admitted into
the castle, was even then under pretended fear
kept close all the day in the porter's lodge.
But at night, being for more security disguised
in lay habit, he was brought into the great
hall, where he beheld one clothed in royal
habiliments to personate a king. The friar
himself, either deceived by the glimmering of
the lamps, or the distance which he was forced
to keep, or the strength of prejudice working
on his fancy, did really take him for the father
of the young king, as he sat with seeming
majesty and princely attendants at a royal
supper.

This account the friar brought back to the
Earl of Kent, persuaded the unfortunate prince
that he had seen, with his own eyes, the king
his brother, alive and well, and at supper.

At the time when the rumour had first
begun to go abroad with some authority, Earl
Edmund, having some occasion at the Court
of Rome, held a discourse at Avignon with
Pope John XXII. After their business was
finished, he desired counsel of his holiness,
touching a matter relating to Edward of
Caernarvon his brother, late King of England,
since was a common fame through England
that he was alive and well.

When the Pope heard this he commanded

the earl upon his blessing to help with all the
power that he might, to deliver him out of
prison and to save his body to the utmost of
his ability, in order to which he assoiled him
and all his partakers with plenary absolution,
and promised to bear the charges of the whole
undertaking, threatening him also with
excommunication if he did not make use of
his best endeavours to assert his brother's
right and liberty.

Soon after Earl Edmund returned to
England, he went himself to Corfe Castle, and
spake with the constable thereof, Sir John
Daverill, and after many rich presents, desired
secretly to know of him whether the late king
was yet alive, or dead. And, if he were alive,
that he might have sight of him.

Sir John Daverill, being Mortimer's creature
answered that indeed his brother was in
health and under his keeping, but that he
durst not show him to any man living, since
he was forbid, in behalf of the king now
reigning, and also of the Queen Mother and of
Mortimer, to show his person to anyone
whatsoever, except only to them.

Earl Edmund was so far deceived by the
constable's protestations, that he delivered to
him a letter, desiring him to bear it to his
brother, which he promised to do.

Soon after the constable carried it to
Mortimer, sealed with the earl's seal. It began
thus:

> 'To the noble knight, Edward of
> Caernarvon, Edmund of Woodstock,
> worship and reverence with
> brotherly allegiance and subjection:
> Sir knight, worshipful and dear
> brother; if it please you, I pray
> heartily that you be of good

comfort, for I shall so ordain for
you that you shall soon come out
of prison and be delivered of that
trouble which you are in; and may
your highness understand that I
have unto me assenting, almost all
the great men of England, with all
their apparel, that it is say with
armour and treasure exceeding
much, for to maintain and help
your quarrel so far forth that you
shall be king again as you were
before; and thereto they have all
sworn to me upon a book, as well
prelates as earls and barons.'

This letter was immediately carried by
Mortimer to the queen who showed it to the
king her son, magnifying his danger from his
uncle's practices. It was not difficult for her
to obtain the king's leave to secure the prince's
person, and as soon as he had given his assent,
the Earl of Kent was apprehended at
Winchester where the Parliament was then
assembled. His impeachment being brought
before the peers, his own letter was produced,
and he could not disown it.

Several lords, the Archbishop of York, and
Bishop of London, were concerned with him,
as he said, in the plot, and that they had
assured him of 5,000 men to assist in it.

He was condemned to be executed. He was **A.D. 1329**
brought upon the scaffold on the 9th of March **9th March**
in the year 1329. There was no executioner **Death of**
to be found. He who had been engaged for **Earl of Kent**
that horrid office went secretly away, and **brother of**
from noon till evening no one could be found **Edward III**
to perform it, so much was the earl beloved.

At last towards night, a condemned
criminal, on promise of his own life being

spared, came to the scaffold and beheaded the unfortunate prince. He died in the 28th year of his age, leaving two sons and two daughters, the youngest of whom was afterwards the most celebrated beauty of her day. She was called 'the beautiful Countess of Kent', and married for her second husband, her cousin, Edward the Black Prince.

House of Lancaster 1399-1461

A.D. 1377
Richard II

In the reign of Richard II, who was the son of the beautiful Countess of Kent, Corfe Castle was possessed unmolested by Thomas Holland, Earl of Kent, and Alicia his wife, near relatives of the king.

A.D. 1399
Henry IV
to
A.D. 1413
Henry V
to
A.D. 1422
Henry VI

After their deaths, Henry IV made a grant of this royal property to the Earl of Somerset, the head of the House of Beaufort, in whose family it continued until the reign of Henry VI.

The Wars of the Roses did not reach the walls of Corfe, but the owner was involved, and at last overwhelmed in the ruin of the Lancastrian party.

The title of duke was now borne by the head of this family, and when Queen Margaret, wife of Henry VI landed at Weymouth on 14th April, 1471, with her party, The Duke of Somerset joined her, and took command. Her son, Edward, Prince of Wales, then 18 years of age, being nominally the leader of the forces.

Wars of
Roses
1455-87

On that very day the terrible battle of Barnet was fought. The Earl of Warwick, and his brother the Marquis of Montacute, with 10,000 men numbering the slain on both sides, perished. Their loss to the Lancastrian party was irreparable. The queen swooned when the news reached her, and would have retired again to France, or at any rate sent her son there for safety.

But the Duke of Somerset persuaded her to the contrary. She took refuge at Beaulieu Abbey in Hampshire, where the Earls of Pembroke and Devonshire, with Lord Wenlock and John Beaufort (brother of the Duke of Somerset) came to her aid.

It is remarkable with what expedition armies were in those days raised. On the 27th April, thirteen days after the Battle of Barnet, the Lancastrian lords had reassembled a considerable army out of the counties of Somerset, Dorset, Wiltshire, Devon and Cornwall. They marched to Gloucester and thence to Tewkesbury, where the battle was fought which sealed the fate of Queen Margaret's party.

She became a prisoner in the Tower, and her son was barbarously murdered. This battle was fought on the 4th May. Two days afterwards the Duke of Somerset, with others that were made prisoners, were publicly beheaded in the market-place of Tewkesbury. The duke's forfeited estates, including the castle and royal domains of Corfe, were now granted to the king's brother, George, Duke of Clarence.

But he held them for no long period, being attainted by the Parliament at Westminster in January, 1478, and committed to the Tower, where he was drowned in a butt of malmsey on February 18th.

Corfe Castle now again reverted to the crown.

Roses

A.D. 1478 Corfe Castle again reverted to the Crown

House of York 1461-1485

**A.D. 1483
Richard III
began to
reign
Death in
A.D. 1485**

Richard III made himself King of England in 1483 by a succession of wicked acts and intrigues, removing obstacles from his path by murder without compunction whenever he deemed such a course desirable.

PART FOUR
Tudors 1485-1603

**A.D. 1485
Henry VII
began to
reign**

When he was deposed and killed, and the rival roses were united on the throne of Henry VII, this king immediately prepared Corfe Castle as a suitable habitation for the residence of his mother, the Countess of Richmond and Derby. His political obligations to her were no less strong than the ties of natural affection.

She had presided over his early education. Remaining in England when he was driven into exile, she watched over his fortunes and gave him notice from time to time of danger which impended over him.

On one occasion, Henry, then Earl of Richmond, had intended to conduct his invasion by landing within sight of this castle, in Poole harbour. He entered the port, but retired in consequence of intelligence that was conveyed to him. He would have perished if he had at that time made the attempt, for the army which the Duke of Buckingham had raised to join with Henry, was destroyed, and the Duke himself was taken and executed at Salisbury, where his body was later discovered.

The Countess of Richmond, mother of the king, had early ties of attachment to the county of Dorset. The first years of her

A young man

40

life were passed at Kingston Lacy, near Wimborne, which then belonged to her parents the Duke and Duchess of Somerset. To their memory she erected a noble monument in the minster of that town. And a still nobler memorial she also planted there, a school, which though it bears the name of Queen Elizabeth, was built and endowed by Lady Margaret, earlier by three generations.

Hawking

In the time of Henry VII the age of defensive castles had passed away. A style of decorative architecture was then introduced which encouraged the lavish expenditure of the great and the rich, so pleasing to the observation of the politic king, who received in his coffers large supplies from the various channels of profusion now opening throughout his kingdom.

He applied no Tudor decoration to Corfe Castle, but preserved, when he gave the necessary reparations, the noble character in all its Saxon strength and Norman grandeur.

The Countess of Richmond outlived the king, her son, by one year.

At her death the possession, reverting to the crown, became the property of King Henry VIII.

A.D. 1509 Corfe reverted to the Crown Henry VIII's reign began

By now abbeys and monasteries were the objects coveted by the great. No courtier would desire to move far from the seat where plunder was distributed, as to the sea-girt Isle of Purbeck. So Corfe remained unappropriated.

A.D. 1547 Death of Henry VIII

But when Henry died, and the proud Seymour, Earl of Hertford became protector, with the title of Duke of Somerset, in behalf of his nephew, King Edward VI, his grasping hand closed upon this royal castle, as it did also upon so vast an amount of religious and other

also Seymour Earl of Hertford Protector for Edward VI

41

royal property throughout the land.

His right of possession continued but few years. Repeatedly assailed by political foes in the turbulent reign of that amiable prince for whom he governed, this duke was brought to trial in December, 1552, and though acquitted of treason, was found guilty of felony, and beheaded on Tower Hill in the month of January following. So once again the castle lapsed to the crown.

In the days of Queen Elizabeth a splendid inhabitant appeared in Corfe. The castle was granted in as full and ample a manner as the terms of law could devise, to her courtly favourite, Sir Christopher Hatton, for him and his heirs. He repaired and decorated this royal gift of Corfe Castle at vast expense, suitable to the high station in life, which he attained.

He was born of a family more ancient than wealthy, in Northamptonshire. Being young, and of a comely tallness of body and amiable countenance, he got into such favour with the queen that she took him into her band of fifty Gentlemen Pensioners; and afterwards, for his modest sweetness of condition, into the number of the Gentlemen of her Privy Chamber. She made him captain of her guard, Vice-Chamberlain, and one of her Privy Council. Lastly she made him Lord Chancellor of England, and honoured him with the Order of Saint George. He was a man of pious nature, and great reliever of the poor, of singular bounty to students and learned men (for which reason those of Oxford chose him Chancellor of their university). He was one who in the execution of that high and weighty office of Lord Chancellor, could satisfy his conscience in the constant integrity of his endeavours to do all

A.D. 1552-53
Protector on trial and beheaded

A.D. 1558
Reign of Elizabeth I commenced

In the 14th year of her reign Corfe granted to Sir Christopher Hatton

A.D. 1578
Sir Christopher made Lord Chancellor

42

with right and equity.

At this the great lawyers of England took very great distaste (says Camden) for, ever since the ecclesiastical men were put aside from this preferment, lawyers had, with singular commendation for their equity and wisdom, borne this highest place of crowned dignity. But Hatton was advanced to it by the cunning court acts of some, intending that by his absence from court, and the troublesome discharge of so great a place, which they thought him not able to undergo—his favour with the queen might flag and grow less.

Yet executed he that place with the greatest state and splendour of any that ever we saw. What he wanted in the knowledge of the law, he laboured to make good by equity and justice.

The same learned writer (Camden) tells us that we are now come to the year of Christ one thousand five hundred eighty eight. An astronomer of Kiningsberg, above an hundred years before, foretold it would be an admirable year. Rumours of wars, which before were but slight and small, began now to grow greater daily. Reports were no longer uncertain. The unanimous belief of all men carried it for certain truth, that a most invincible armada was rigged and prepared in Spain against England, and that the famousest captains and expertest leaders and soldiers were sent from Italy, Sicily, yea, and out of America into Spain.

A.D. 1588 Armada set sail from Spain

Corfe was now again to become a fortress. The coasts of Cornwall, Devonshire,

The first castles were wooden towers with defences

43

Dorsetshire, and the Isle of Wight were considered to be the first points of attack. Cannon were for the first time mounted in this castle.

The queen for encouragement gave a charter to the inhabitants of the castle and borough, which conferred upon them all the same rights and privileges as those enjoyed by the inhabitants and barons of the Cinque Ports, including the right of returning two members to Parliament.

The Armada did, in fact, pass within a short distance of the Dorsetshire coast, also of the southern extremity of the Isle of Wight. But so far was it from terrifying those who dwelt there, with its name *Invincible*, that the young gentry of England, with incredible cheerfulness and alacrity, out of their hearty love to their country, hired ships from all parts at their own private charges, and joined with the fleet in great numbers.

A countrywoman

William Hatton, a nephew of the Lord Chancellor, with many more of the highest rank, became efficient members of this yacht club, so gallantly and rapidly established.

In the year 1591 the health of Sir Christopher Hatton declined. He had ailments of the body, together with grief of mind. The queen had somewhat rigorously exacted of him a great sum of money collected of tenths and first fruits, whereof he had the charge, and which he hoped—in regard of the favour he was in with her—she would have forgiven him.

Neither could she, having once cast him down with a harsh word, raise him up again, though she visited and endeavoured to comfort him. His funeral was honourably performed at Paul's Church in London. Sir

Christopher Hatton had lived unmarried. At his death Corfe Castle passed to his nephew, Sir William Hatton, son of Sir Christopher's sister.

A.D. 1597
Death of Sir
Christopher
Hatton

This knight, Sir William, left no children, and ultimately the property came to his widow, the Lady Elizabeth Hatton, daughter of Thomas Cecil, Earl of Exeter.

Sovereigns preceding Elizabeth, when alienating this royal property, had inserted as a condition of their grant, a proviso for rights of the crown. This secured to themselves or to their successors a reversion, under circumstances which were prescribed in the gift.

Elizabeth found it a more frugal and agreeable plan to enjoy the castles and fair mansions of her kingdom at the cost of her wealthy subjects rather than her own. They were justly proud of the high privilege of receiving her.

The widow of Sir William Hatton, who now possessed the castle, was renowned for her beauty as well as for the large fortune of which she was possessed. Her first husband dying in the year 1597, she received proposals, within a very short time, from Francis Bacon, whose brilliant professional career was then very generally anticipated. His great talents and acquirements were well known, though his prospects had been thwarted by every method that it was in the power of his jealous rival, Sir Edward Coke, to resort to.

Bacon is said to have implored the intercession of the powerful patron whom he so soon afterwards basely forsook—the Earl of Essex—to aid him in his suit. But neither the lady herself, nor any of her relations, the Cecils, were induced to give any countenance

45

to this proposition. It could be no matter for surprise that a young lady, endowed with great personal personal beauty, and possessed of large revenues, including a splendid residence in the country, and the noble mansion erected by Sir Christopher Hatton in London, should entertain higher views than those of a briefless barrister, however rich he might be in mental powers.

A.D. 1598-99 But when the successful suitor was declared, astonishment pervaded the whole court.

On the 27th of June, in the year 1598 Sir Edward Coke had the misfortune to lose a beloved wife in the 34th year of her age. She had brought to him some considerable property, and died at the house which was her own in the county of Suffolk, leaving to him several children.

On the 24th of November in the same year, Sir Edward Coke, Attorney-General, in the evening, in a private house, without licence or banns, married the Lady Hatton, in the presence of her father Lord Burghley, who gave her away.

The very circumstances of the marriage were a commencement to matrimonial troubles. The bride would only consent to a marriage under circumstances which were well known to be illegal, and likely to be severely censured and liable for punishment in the ecclesiastical courts. As to an appearance in church with such an elderly bridegroom—it was not to be mentioned to Lady Hatton. The love of secrecy and mystery prominent in her wayward character forbade a resort either to banns or licence, and this at a time when the church had become particularly vigilant in exacting at least one of these preliminaries as essential to marriage rites.

46

The attorney-general's irregular marriage produced in consequence a citation from the Ecclesiastical Court, including his bride, Lord Burghley, and the minister who performed the ceremony. They were subjected to a train of legal proceedings terminating in a sentence of the greater excommunication.

Thus circumstanced, Mr Attorney had no other course to pursue, than by a plea for mercy on the ground of total ignorance of the Ecclesiastical Law.

So commenced the honeymoon of this newly married pair. The lady would not consent to take her husband's name, nor would she permit him to enter her fine house in Holborn publicly. When he called there it must be at a back door. In truth he was glad again to resort to the old comforts of his chambers in the Temple. Memoirs of this lady who by her second marriage became wife of the Lord Chief Justice Coke (to whose domestic happiness she by no means contributed!) take their place in the many extraordinary private histories of the court of James I.

Early in the reign of James I, Sir Edward Coke became Chief Justice of the Common Pleas. He presided there from June 1606 until October 1613. He was then, to his infinite displeasure, promoted, and appointed to the higher office of Chief Justice of the King's Bench—an office, though of superior rank, very much inferior in emolument.

A.D. 1603
James I
reign began

Meantime his new wife had presented him with a daughter.

Coke's seeming promotion was brought about by the contrivance of Bacon, now become Attorney-General.

47

PART FIVE
Stuarts 1603-1649

In the year 1616 Bacon, determining to
take down something from the height of his
old rival, procured that Coke should be
summoned before the Privy Council, to
answer certain charges preferred against him.
He was suspended from the office of chief
justice. The terms of the decree of the Privy
Council signified that he would now have
time privately to dispose of himself at home.
But he had no home. The Lady Hatton had
divided herself from him, disfurnishing his
house in Holborn and at Stoke, of all within
them, retiring herself to some obscure place.

A.D. 1616
Lady Hatton

It is not improbable that Corfe Castle was
at this time honoured by Lady Hatton's
presence. She was extremely fond of such
noble sports of the field as might be pursued
there. Hawking especially was one of her
delights.

She was not, however, pleased with the
degradation of her husband, much as she
despised him. She now quarrelled with both
the king and the queen for his sake. She had
been on very intimate terms of friendship with
the queen, but she was now forbidden the
court.

A.D. 1617
Lady Frances

In the year 1617 their daughter, the Lady
Frances, became a source of new and
aggravated disquiet to this ill-matched pair.
Sir Edward saw in this daughter a chance of
success in regard to the first wish of his
heart—the humiliation of his rival Bacon, and
hopefully of his own reinstatement in dignity
and power.

The Lady Frances was at this time only
fourteen years old. She was a very rich

48

heiress (her mother's large possessions being entailed upon her). She might also expect a share in the immense wealth accumulated by her father.

This little girl had also inherited the beauty of her mother. She had attracted the notice of the Duke of Buckingham's elder brother, Sir John Villiers; nearly thrice her age, and exceedingly poor.

Sir Edward Coke, while Chief Justice, had scorned the idea of such a match, but now he entertained the notion of supplanting his hated rival the Lord Chancellor, making use of his own daughter as his instrument.

The child and her fortune were to be given as the price of her father's restoration to power. Sir Edward might not perhaps have known where to find his wife at the time when the contract was entered into—but all matters were arranged without consulting either Lady Hatton of her daughter.

When the matter came at last to her notice the Lady Hatton broke forth into frantic passion that such an important arrangement had been made in the family without her previous knowledge and permission.

A gentleman

When the fury of her anger was in some degree spent, Sir Edward went to bed.

Lady Hatton left him to enjoy his slumbers, and stepping forth with her daughter into a coach which she had prepared, they travelled all night, arriving in the morning at Oatlands, which was then rented by a cousin of Lady Hatton. For a time they stayed concealed there, during which time Lady Hatton exerted all her influence to deter her daughter from the intended marriage, even forging letters— as from other persons—who she said aspired to her daughter's hand.

49

When their retreat was discovered, Sir Edward applied to the Privy Council for a search-warrant. This he was not able to obtain. At last he found no other expedient than to go himself at the head of an armed party, he himself being armed, to demand the restitution of his child. Oatlands stood a seige on this occasion of some hours. At last an entry was effected through a window, and the Lady Frances, being seized, forcibly carried away to Stoke Pogis, the dismantled mansion of Lady Hatton. There Sir Edward secured her in an upper chamber, himself keeping the key.

The Lord Chancellor, now fully aware of Coke's plot, strongly encouraged Lady Hatton in her resistance to the proposed match. Various steps were taken by the Lord Chancellor, and the Attorney-General, and at the same time Lady Hatton attempted to recover possession of her daughter by forcible means. She failed, and was imprisoned by procurement of her husband for this attempt.

On Michaelmas Day in the year 1617 the marriage was eventually celebrated at Hampton Court Palace, in the presence of the king and queen, and all the chief nobility of England. Lady Hatton was still in confinement, and Sir Edward came therefore unmolested. The bridal banquet was most splendid, and a masque was performed in the evening, followed by all the usual nuptial ceremonials of that period.

Sir Edward Coke was now restored to the Privy Council, but he derived no other advantage from the sacrifice of his daughter.

His rival Bacon was re-established. But, far worse, Lady Hatton being now set at liberty, became the delight of the whole court. The

king and queen accepted a grand entertainment
from her at Hatton House in Holborn, to
which not only was Sir Edward not invited,
but he and all his servants expressly excluded.

Sir John Villiers was, in June 1619, created
Viscount Purbeck, in the County of Dorset,
in right of his wife's expected property. Lady
Hatton appears to have called Corfe Castle by,
the name of Purbeck Castle, and to have
considered the whole of that island as her
own.

**A.D. 1619
Sir John
Villiers
created
Viscount
Purbeck**

The gaieties of the court received a severe
check when the queen died, aged 44, in the
month of March, 1619.

Denmark House, the late queen's residence,
was now assigned to the Prince of Wales. But
the little queen of fashion, Lady Purbeck,
daughter of Lady Hatton, and wife of Sir
John Villiers—was permitted to have the care
of it, and to reside there.

All during the reign of James I, the
domestic quarrels between Lady Elizabeth
Hatton and Sir Edward Coke, and the Lady
Frances and Lord Purbeck, remained in full
vigour. Persons of the highest quality ranged
themselves on the one side or the other. The
courtiers of James I were divided into factions
on the quarrels of the daughter with her
husband, as they had heretofore been in the
disputes betwixt her father and her mother.

**A.D. 1603-25
Reign of
James I**

The Duke of Buckingham was especially
desirous that his sister-in-law should do public
penance in a white sheet. He procured a
sentence in the Ecclesiastical Court, awarding
that punishment for her delinquencies. But it
was by no means easy to catch her. She
assumed male attire as readily as she did that
of her own sex, looking equally well in both.

On one occasion she was very nearly

captured near the residence of one of the foreign ambassadors. But the pages of his excellency, delighted with the frolic, dressed up one of their own fraternity in a girl's clothes, putting him into a coach which drove furiously along the Strand, pursued as rapidly by the officers of justice—in the midst of an enormous concourse of people which had collected. When the capture was effected, they found it was the postmaster's boy!

At the death of James I, the subject of such excitement was not exhausted.

Sir Edward Coke died on 3rd September, 1634, in the 83rd year of his age.

Ten years after the accession of Charles I, in 1635, a letter from the Rev. G. Garrard to the Earl of Strafford, contains among other news of the day:

> 'Here is a business new revived;
> Your Lordship hath heard of a strong
> friendship betwixt Sir Robert
> Howard and the Lady Purbeck, for
> which she was called into the High
> Commission, and there sentenced
> to stand in a sheet in the Savoy
> Church, which she avoided then
> by flight, and hath not been much
> looked after since, having lived
> much out of town, and constantly
> these last two years with her father
> at Stoke until he died.
>
> This winter she lodged herself on
> the water-side over against Lambeth,
> I fear too near the road of the
> Archbishop's barge. Whereof, some
> complaint being made, she had a
> serjeant-at-arms sent with a warrant
> from the Lords of the Council to
> carry her to the Gatehouse, whence

A.D. 1625
Death of
James I
A.D. 1625
Reign of
Charles I
commenced
A.D. 1634
Death of Sir
Edward Coke
A.D. 1635
News of
Lady
Purbeck

52

she will hardly get out until she
have done the penance. The same
night was a warrant sent, signed by
the Lords, to the warden of the
Fleet.'

17th March, 1635,
St. Patrick's Day.
Sir Edward's only domestic solace we are
told, was the company of his daughter, Lady
Purbeck, whom he had forgiven, and she
continued piously to watch over him until his
death. Other letters written by Mr. Garrard
contained information about persons who fall
within the scope of this narrative, and an
extract is given:

'No news yet of the Lady Purbeck
since her escape out of the
Gatehouse.

Sir Robert Howard lies by it still,
close prisoner in the Fleet, being so
committed by the High Common
Court until he shall bring her forth
. . . like to pay dear for his unlawful
pleasures.

Shall I tell yourself how Bankes
the Attorney-General hath been
commended unto his Majesty—that
he exceeds Bacon in eloquence,
Chancellor Ellesmere in judgment,
and William Noy in law? High
praises.'

When Sir Edward Coke died, his widow and
daughter found themselves at liberty to
dispose of a mansion whose gloomy grandeur
and position remote from the busier scenes of
life could not well accord with their tastes and
habits. The very entrance of the castle with
its massive barriers and ponderous portcullis,
could hardly fail to remind these ladies of the

Gatehouse, in which each of them had passed a portion of her time not very agreeably.

**A.D. 1634
Corfe Castle
sold to Sir
John Bankes**

Sir John Bankes, knighted in 1634, Attorney-General 1640 and Chief Justice of the Common Pleas, became at this period the proprietor of Corfe Castle. It may appear a matter for surprise that a private gentleman whose habits and disposition were such as have been described, should have made purchase of a palace for his place of residence. Also that the profession of the law should have enabled a practitioner, however able and diligent, at a comparatively early period of life, to possess himself not only of this large mansion and domain, but of an extent of lands purchased in addition in other parts of the same county, adequate for maintaining it.

The biographers of men eminent in the law during this period observed that their gains were due to the smaller numbers of legal practitioners engaged in the law, as compared with the very ample supply of barristers in this honourable profession at a later date.

The new Attorney-General had not attained his elevated position as a flatterer nor by any unseemly intrigues or courtly struggles. He hoped in this retirement to find a happy relaxation from the toils of public life. The retired situation of Corfe Castle, and the salubrity of soil and climate, were inducements to Sir John. But it was not to be. The position he had so honourably attained, without envy or hatred from any quarter, became on a sudden a post surrounded by dangers, difficulties, and contentions of the bitterest and most anxious description. The peaceful dwelling which he had earned with years of toil, and purchased for his children's home, became the scene of battle, siege, and death.

For we have now arrived at a period when
Corfe Castle again takes its place in the
annals of the kingdom, and the lady, the
inhabitant at this date, who has justly been
styled the heroine of Corfe Castle, must be
introduced to those who may wish to hear
more of its story.

This lady, wife of Sir John Bankes, was a
daughter of the very ancient family of the
Hawtreys, whose place of residence was at
Ruislip, in the county of Middlesex. They
were of Norman descent, having come into
this country at the time of the Conquest.
A large portion of the flat pavement of the
church at Ruislip consists of the tombs of the
different generations of the Hawtreys. We can
furnish no more full or faithful account of
the proceedings of this brave lady than by
giving them as related in the words of the
well-known diurnal of the day *The Mercurius
Rusticus:*

"There is in the Isle of Purbeck a strong
castle called Corfe Castle, seated on a very
steep hill, in the fracture of a hill in the very
midst of it, being eight miles in length,
running from the east end of the peninsula to
the west; and though it stands between the
two ends of this fracture, so that it might
seem to lose much advantage of its natural and
artificial strength as commanded from thence,
being in height equal to, if not overlooking,
the tops of the highest towers of the castle;
yet the structure of the castle is so strong, the
ascent so steep, the walls so massive and
thick, that it is one of the impregnablest forts
of the kingdom, and of very great
concernment in respect of its command over
the island and the places about it.

"This castle is now in the possession and

inheritance of the Right Honourable Sir John Bankes, Chief Justice of the Common Pleas, and one of His Majesty's most Honourable Privy Council, who, receiving commands from the king to attend him at York in Easter Term, 1642, had leave from the two houses to obey his commands.

"After the unhappy differences between the king and the two houses, or rather between the king and the action in both houses, grew high, it being generally feared that the sword would decide the controversy; the Lady Bankes, a virtuous and prudent lady, resolved, with her children and family, to retire to this castle, there to shelter themselves from the storm which she saw coming, which accordingly she did. There she and her family remained in peace all the winter and a great part of the spring until May, 1643, about which time the rebels, under the command of Sir Walter Erle, Sir Thomas Trenchard, and others, had possessed themselves of Dorchester, Lyme, Melcombe, Weymouth, Wareham, and Poole (Portland Castle being treacherously delivered to the rebels), only Corfe Castle remaining in obedience to the king. But the rebels, knowing how much it concerned them to add this castle to their other garrisons, to make all the sea-coast wholly for them, and thinking it more feasible to take it by treachery than open hostility, resolved to lay hold of an opportunity coming on, to see if they could become masters of it.

"There is an ancient usage that the Mayor and Barons, as they call them, of Corfe Castle, accompanied by the gentry of the island, have permission from the lord of the castle, on May-day, to course a stag, which every year is performed with much solemnity and great

A.D. 1643 Rebels— under command of Sir Walter Erle and others

concourse of people.

"On this day some troops of horse from Dorchester and other places came into the island, intending to find other game than to hunt the stag, their business being suddenly to surprise the gentlemen in the hunting, and to take the castle. The news of their coming dispersed the hunters and spoiled the sport of that day, and made the Lady Bankes to give order for the safe custody of the castle gates, and to keep them shut against all comers.

A.D. 1643
1st May
Lady Mary
Bankes
closed gates
of Corfe
Castle

"The troopers having missed their prey on the hills (the gentlemen having withdrawn themselves), some of them came to the castle under a pretence to see it, but, entrance being denied them, the common soldiers used threatening language, casting out words implying some intentions to take the castle. But the commanders (who know better how to conceal their resolutions) utterly disavowed any such thought, denying that they had any such commission.

"However, the Lady Bankes, very wisely, and like herself, hence took occasion to call in a guard to assist her, not knowing how soon she might have occasion to make use of them, it being now more than probable that the rebels had a design upon the castle.

"The taking in of this guard, as it *secured* her at *home*, so it rendered her suspected abroad. From thenceforward there was a watchful and vigilant eye to survey all her actions. Whatsoever she sends out, or sends for in, is suspected. Her ordinary provisions for her family are by fame multiplied and reported to be more than double what indeed they were; as if she now had an intention to victual and man the castle against the forces of the two Houses of Parliament!

57

'Small pieces' were the cannon

"Presently letters are sent from the Committee at Poole to demand the four small pieces in the castle, and the pretence was because the islanders conceived strange jealousies that the pieces were mounted and put on their carriages.

"Hereupon the Lady Bankes despatched messengers to Dorchester and Poole, to entreat the Commissioners that the small pieces might remain in the castle for her own defence. To take away the ground of the islanders jealousies, she caused the pieces to be taken off their carriages again. Hereupon a promise was made that they should be left to her possession. But there passed not many days before forty seamen (they in the castle not suspecting any such thing) came very early in the morning to demand the pieces. The lady in person (early as it was) goes to the gates, and desires to see their warrant. They produced one, under the hands of some of the Commissioners.

A cannon

"But instead of delivering them, though at the time there were but five men in the castle, yet these five, assisted by the maidservants, at their lady's command, mount these pieces on their carriages again, and loading one of them, they gave fire, which small thunder so affrighted the seamen that they all quitted the castle and ran away!

"They being gone, by beat of drum she summons help into the castle, and upon the alarm given a very considerable guard of tenants and friends came in to her assistance, there being withal some fifty arms brought into the castle from several parts of the island; this guard was kept in the castle about a week. During this time many threatening letters were sent unto the lady, telling her what great forces should be sent to fetch them if she would not by fair means be persuaded to deliver them; and to deprive her of her auxiliaries, all or most of them being neighbours thereabouts, they threaten that, if they oppose the delivery of them, they would fire their houses. Presently their wives come to the castle, there they weep and wring their hands, and with clamorous oratory persuade their husbands to come home, and not by saving others to expose their own houses to spoil and ruin.

"Now to reduce the castle into a distressed condition they did not only intercept two hundredweight of powder, provided against a siege, but they interdict them the liberty of common markets. Proclamation is made at Wareham (a market-town hard by) that no beef, beer, or other provisions should be sold to Lady Bankes, or for her use; strict watches are kept that no messenger shall pass into or out of the castle. Being thus distressed, all means of victualling the castle being taken away, and being but slenderly furnished for a siege, either with ammunition or with victual, at last they came to a treaty of composition, of which the result was that the Lady Bankes should deliver up those four small pieces, the biggest carrying not above a three-pound bullet, and that the rebels should permit her to enjoy the castle and arms in it in peace and quietness.

"And though this wise lady knew too well to rest satisfied or secured in these promises (their often breach of faith having sufficiently instructed her what she might expect from them), yet she was glad of this opportunity to strengthen herself even by that means by which many in the world thought she had

Wives come to the castle

'Treaty of Composition'

done herself much prejudice; for the rebels, being now possessed of their guns presumed the castle to be theirs, as sure as if they had actually possessed it.

"Now it was no more but ask and have. Hereupon they grew remiss in their watches, negligent in their observations; not heeding what was brought in, nor taking care as before, to intercept supplies which might enable them to hold out against a siege. And the lady, making good use of this remissness, laid hold on the present opportunity, and as much as the time would permit furnished the castle with provisions of all sorts. In this interval there was brought in an hundred and a half of powder, and a quantity of match proportionable.

Lady Mary appeals for help

"And understanding that the king's forces, under the conduct of Prince Maurice and the Marquis of Hertford, were advancing towards Blandford she, by her messenger, made her address to them to signify unto them the present condition in which they were, the great consequence of the place, desiring their assistance, and in particular that they would be pleased to take into their serious consideration to send some commanders thither to take charge of the castle. Hereupon

Captain Lawrence to the rescue

they send Captain Lawrence, son of Sir Edward Lawrence, a gentleman of that island, to Command in Chief. But he, coming without a Commission, could not command moneyes or provisions to be brought in until it was too late.

"There was likewise in the castle one Captain Bond, an old soldier, whom I should deprive of his due honour not to mention him, having shared in the honour of this resistance. The first time the rebels faced the

60

castle they brought a body of between two and three hundred horse and foot, and two pieces of ordnance, and from the hills played on the castle, fired four houses in the town, and then summoned the castle; but receiving a denial for that time, they left it.

"But on the three-and-twentieth of June the sagacious knight Sir Walter Erle (that hath the gift of discerning treasons, and might have made up his nine-and-thirty treasons forty, by reckoning in his own), accompanied by Captain Sidenham, Captain Henry Jarvis, Captain Skuts, son of the arch-traitor Skuts of Poole, with a body of between five and six hundred, came and possessed themselves of the the town, taking the opportunity of a misty morning, that they might find no resistance from the castle.

"They brought with them to the siege a demi-canon, a culveris, and two sacres. With these and their small shot they played on the castle on all quarters of it with good observation of advantages, making their battery strongest where they thought the castle weakest. And to bind the soldiers by tie of conscience to an eager prosecution of the siege, they administer them an oath and mutually bind themselves to most unchristian resolutions, that, if they found the defendants obstinate not to yield, they would maintain the siege to victory, and then deny quarter unto all, killing without mercy men, women, and children. And to bring on their own soldiers they abused them with falsehoods telling them that the castle stood on a level, yet with good advantages of approach; that there were but forty men in the castle, whereof twenty were for them; that there was rich booty and the like. So during the siege

Sir Walter
Erle takes
the town of
Corfe
The Castle
stands firm

Stone thrower

61

they used all base unworthy means to corrupt the defendants to betray the castle into their hands. The better sort they endeavour to corrupt with bribes, to the rest they offer double pay and the whole plunder of the castle.

"When all these arts took no effect, then they fall to stratagems and engines; one they call the 'sow', and the other the 'boar', being made with boards lined with wool to dead the shot. The first that moved forward was the sow, but not being musket-proof she cast nine of eleven of her farrow; for the musketiers from this castle were so good marksmen at their legs, the only part of their bodies left without defence, that nine ran away as well as their broken and battered legs would give them leave. And of the two which knew neither how to run away, nor well to stay for fear, one was slain.

"The boar, one of the two (a man would think), the valianter creature, seeing the ill success of the sow to cast her litter before her time, durst not advance. The most advantageous part of their batteries was the church, which they without fear of profanation used, not only as their rampart but their rendezvous. Of the surplice they made two shirts for two soldiers; they broke down the organ and made the pipes serve for cases to hold their powder and shot; and not being furnished with musket-bullets, they cut off the lead of the church and rolled it up to shoot it without ever casting it in a mould.

"Sir Walter and the commanders were earnest to press forward the soldiers, but, as prodigal as they were of the blood of the common soldiers, they were sparing enough of their own. It was a general observation that

The 'Boar' and the 'Sow'

Stratagems and engines

valiant Sir Walter never willingly exposed
himself to any hazard, for, being by chance
endangered with a bullet-shot through his
coat, afterwards he put on a bear's skin; and
to the eternal honour of this knight's valour
be it recorded, for fear of musket shot (for
others they had none), he was seen to creep
on all fours on the sides of the hill to keep
himself from danger. This base cowardice of
the assailants added courage and resolution to
the defendants. Therefore, not compelled by
want, but rather to brave the rebels, they
sallied out and brought in either cows or a
bull into the castle without the loss of a man
or a man wounded. At another time five boys
fetched in four cows. They that stood on the
hills called to one in a house in the valley,
crying: 'Shoot, Anthony.' But Anthony
thought good to sleep in a whole skin and
durst not look out, so that afterwards it grew
into a proverbial jeer from the defendants to
the assailants: 'Shoot, Anthony!'

*Sir Walter and
the bear skin*

"The rebels having spent much time and
ammunition, and some men, and yet being as
far from hopes of taking the castle as the first
day they came thither, at last the Earl of
Warwick sends them a supply of an hundred
and fifty mariners, with several cart-loads of
petards, grannadoes, and other warlike
provisions, with scaling-ladders to assault the
castle by scaladoe. They make large offers to
him who shall first scale the wall—twenty
pounds to the first, and so by descending
sums a reward to the twentieth; but all this
could not avail with these silly wretches, who
were brought thither, as themselves confessed,
like sheep to the slaughter, some of them
having exchanged the manner of their death,
the halter for the bullet, having taken them

**The Earl of
Warwick
sends the
rebels
reinforcements**

63

out of gaols. One of them being taken prisoner had letters testimonial in his hands whence he came; the letters I mean when he was burnt for a felon, being very visible to the beholders: but when they found that persuasion could not prevail with such abject low spirited men, the commanders resolve on another course, which was to make them drunk, knowing that drunkenness makes some men fight like lions, that being sober would run away like hares. To this purpose they fill them with strong waters, even to madness, and ready they are now for any design; and for fear Sir Walter should be valiant against his will, like Caesar, he was the only man almost that came sober to the assault; an imitation of the Turkish practice (for certainly there can be nothing of Christianity in it, to send poor souls to God's judgment-seat in the very act of two grievous sins, rebellion and drunkenness), who to stupify their soldiers and make them insensible of their dangers, give them opium.

"Being now armed with drink they resolve to storm the castle on all sides and apply their scaling-ladders, it be ordered by the leaders (if I may without a solecism, call them so that stood behind and did not so much as follow) that when twenty were entered they should give a watch-word to the rest, and that was Old Wat, a word ill chosen by Sir Walter Erle, and, considering the business in hand little better than ominous, for if I be not deceived the hunters that beat bushes for the fearful timorous hare call him Old Wat.

Captain Lawrence defends the Middle Ward

"Being now pot-valiant and possessed with a borrowed courage which was to evaporate in sleep, they divide their forces into two parties, whereof one assaults the middle ward, defended by valiant Captain Lawrence a. d the greater part of the soldiers; the other assaults the upper ward, which the Lady Bankes (to her eternal honour be it spoken) with her daughters, women, and five soldiers, undertook to make good against the rebels, and did bravely perform what she undertook; for by heaving over stones and hot embers they repelled the rebels and kept them from climbing the ladders, thence to throw in that wildfire which every rebel had already in his hand.

Lady Mary defends the Upper Ward

"Being repelled, and having in this siege and this assault lost and hurt an hundred men, Old Sir Wat, hearing that the king's forces were advanced, cried and ran away crying, leaving Sydenham to command in chief, to bring off the ordnance, ammunition, and the remainder of the army, who, afraid to appear abroad, kept sanctuary in the church til night, meaning to sup and run away by starlight; but supper being ready and set on the table, an alarm was given that the king's forces were coming.

"This news took away Sydenham's stomach; all this provision was but messes of meat set before the sepulchres of the dead; he leaves his artillery, ammunition, and (with which these men is something) a good supper, and ran away to take a boat to Poole, leaving likewise at the shore about an hundred horse to the next takers, which next day proved a good prize to the soldiers of the castle.

"Thus after six weeks strict siege, this castle, the desire of the rebels, the tears of Old Sir Wat, and the key of those parts, by the loyalty and brave resolution of this honourable lady, the valour of Captain Lawrence, and some eighty soldiers (by the loss only of two men) was delivered from the

Siege lifted after six weeks— 4th August 1643

65

bloody intentions of those merciless rebels on the fourth of August."

**A.D. 1646
Events
leading up to
final betrayal
and
destruction
of the Castle**

Few portions of the kingdom, and not many private families in England were now undisturbed, for the actual presence of civil war, or the rumours of its near approach, shook the domestic happiness as well of the highest as of the humblest classes, and carried grief and apprehension throughout the land.

The king's beloved consort was now become of necessity a queen on horseback, and after many months of separation the royal pair met again, and with joyful hope—but their meeting was on a field of battle.

Sir John Bankes, the grave and learned judge, closing the labours of his circuit, returned after a long absence to his home, and in its battered walls was welcomed by his wife who had become a heroine, and by children who had endless stories to relate of their invincible prowess in the days of danger. He found his castle safe, his property preserved, but the church which stood in front of his castle gate was unroofed and desecrated, the shops in the little town plundered, and all that would burn of the stone-built cottages around destroyed by conflagration.

The poor families thus expelled found their refuge within the walls which they had so faithfully helped to defend.

There was much however to render this a joyful meeting at Corfe Castle, for it seemed as if the sun of the king's fortunes, arrested in its decline, stood still in the west, with a brilliant lustre that gave hope of a better morrow.

The fighting continued. Upon the surrender of Bristol, Dorchester surrendered to the Earl of Caernarvon. Lord Clarendon at this

66

time wrote:

A.D. 1643
Bristol
surrendered
to Prince
Rupert
Dorchester
surrendered
to Earl of
Caernarvon

The fame of the Earl's coming, had before frighted Sir Walter Erle, who had for a long time besieged Corfe Castle (the house of the Lord Chief Justice Bankes, defended by his lady with her servants, and some few gentlemen and tenants, who took themselves thither for her assistance and security), from that siege; and he making more haste to convey himself to London than generals use to do who have the care and charge of others, his forces were presently dispersed; and now the surrender of Dorchester (the magazine from whence the other places were supplied) infused the same spirit into Weymouth, a very convenient harbour and haven. And the example again prevailed on the island and castle of Portland (a place not enough understood, but of wonderful importance), to all which the Earl granted fair conditions, and received them into his Majesty's protection.

The fortifying of London was carried on with unceasing activity. The defences embraced a circuit of twelve miles.

Now the king had to decide how to dispose of the triumphant force which had captured Bristol. The queen had no hesitation in advising an immediate march upon the capital. The parliament fully expected that course would have been taken. It is a striking exception to the supposed unbounded influence of the queen over her husband, which has by almost every writer been recorded to the king's disadvantage, that her advice and entreaties had in this instance no effect.

A.D. 1643
Gloucester
Besieged by
Charles I

On the 10th August the king, nobly attended, arrived before Gloucester. The garrison did not exceed 1500 men; the fortifications, large in extent, were in a very unfinished state; the store of powder very scanty, and provisions not abundant. The city resisted, and its resistance saved London.

Essex had time given him to march to its relief and the celebrity of this exploit gained for him new acclamation, and bound him by additional ties to the cause of Parliament.

On 19th September when approaching Newbury, Essex met the royal army, with the king in person, so posted as to render a battle unavoidable. The irreparable losses to the king in the deaths of three of the noblest and bravest of his supporters Lord Falkland, the Earl of Caernarvon, and the Earl of Sunderland, was the final blow. Exeter and Dartmouth surrendered in September and October.

Early in 1643 a publication had appeared which attracted much attention. Of this a copy is found amongst the papers of Sir John Bankes, which has a multitude of interlineations in his own handwriting, as if in preparation for a second edition. Whether he was principally concerned in the production of this publication is not known; the sentiments herein expressed seem to accord very precisely with those which he entertained. A few extracts are inserted from this work called *The Moderator*:

A.D. 1643
"The
Moderator"

We are now arrived almost to the extremities of ill; and yet some believe that there is a way to grow better by growing worse. I pray Heaven this paradox may not undo us.

The true character of a moderate man I conceive to be this: He is one that could never be so well satisfied of the necessary why this war began as he is now why it should see an end, and who knows not how to pray for victory; one that in earnest loves the king, and thinks him essential to the well being of a Parliament. One that honours, not adores, the Parliament because he sees they also are but men; one that would have his religion nor gaudy nor stripped naked; one that is sorry to see it more seasonable than safe to speak the truth.

'Tis commonly granted that with his Majesty there are the generality of the nobility, gentry, and clergy throughout the whole kingdom, and a great part of the people everywhere, who of late do fall off from the other side every day more and more.

On the Parliament side there are, beside some nobility, gentry, and clergy, the greater part of the commonalty, the corporations, forts, and navy. Nor is it without ground suspected that many of those that fall from them do it to save charges and for fear of future payments.

The war went on. There were no persons now who had any powers to negotiate. In the month of December 1643 the king issued summonses for a meeting of the Parliament at Oxford. Charles was very much perplexed how to maintain the war in the ensuing campaign, knowing what active preparations were proceeding on the side of Parliament.

He sought an expedient to free himself from the difficulty of obtaining further money for the continuance of the war. He assembled at Oxford all the members who had been driven from the Parliament in London, and publicly declared he no longer looked upon those assemblages at Westminster as a Parliament. He did not expect this new Parliament would increase the number of his friends, but he could reasonably hope it would grant him an aid of money, and that, being authorized by such an act, he might openly and by way of authority levy what money was necessary.

A.D. 1643 Charles I summoned Parliament at Oxford in Great Hall of Christ Church

This Parliament assembled in the Great Hall of Christ Church, met in obedience to the royal proclamation on 22nd January 1644. One hundred and eighteen attended. The Parliament sat until 16th April, was then prorogued to the month of October, and never met again. It served only to procure money for the king, and to exhibit a spectacle never before seen in England, namely, two Parliaments at once, holding their sessions at the same time.

The tide of royal success which had flowed so steadily through the western counties in the preceding year, was now ebbing fast in the county of Dorset.

Corfe Castle was now almost the only place of strength between Exeter and London which still held out for the royal cause, and the constant valour of the lady who defended it is to be estimated, not so much by her active enterprise and resistance in the hours of excitement and attack, as by her long endurance through tedious weeks and months of anxiety, encompassed as she was by threats and dangers on every side.

She had now a second gloomy winter to look forward to; all the neighbouring towns had become hostile, and the only encouragement and aid she could expect, her husband being absent and her sons quite young, was that of a garrison to consist of soldiers brought from a distance, under the command of officers who were little, if at all, known to her.

Early in the winter the misfortune which she had least reason to anticipate befell her. On the 28th day of December 1644 her husband, the Chief Justice, died at Oxford. His illness must have been a short one. Whether Lady Bankes had any notice of it is not known, few of her papers having escaped from the plunder of the castle. Sir John Bankes died in the house of his son-in-law, Sir Robert Jenkinson, his two eldest daughters attending him.

A.D. 1644
Death of
Sir John
Bankes

His wife and children were declared malignants on his death, and all property forfeited, this being the price of his loyalty to the king; and the issue of the miserable contest in which his sense of duty had involved him, was now accomplised to this extent, that the king was deprived of every regal power, and there remained to the Parliament nothing but its name.

At York Sir John Bankes had been represented to the king as a faithful but too timid counsellor of the crown. He had now lived long enough to see every one of the fears which he had entertained realised almost to their fullest extent.

Fighting continued. In June at the battle of Naseby the destruction of the royal army was accompanied with the loss of all their artillery and baggage, including even the king's cabinet which contained his most private papers.

Some few places still held out, and Corfe Castle was one of these. It was now in a state of blockade, liable to renewed attacks at any moment.

**A.D. 1645
Battle of
Naseby**

Four days after the battle of Naseby, encouraged by the tidings of that success, Captain Butler, then Governor of Wareham, marched from thence with a party of horse, and, with these driving the garrison into the castle, a company of foot which followed entered the town bent on pillage, and succeeded in bringing away 160 cattle and horses.

Sherborne surrendered to the Parliamentary forces.

Basing House was taken by storm. The blockade of Exeter completed in October, and orders now sent for more effective operations against Corfe Castle.

Colonel Bingham, Governor of Poole, had two regiments placed at his disposal for this purpose, and further reinforcements were sent by General Fairfax.

No expedition more gallant had occurred during the whole course of the civil war than that which was undertaken on the 29th January 1646 by a young officer of the name of Cromwell. Hearing of the distressed condition of a widowed lady shut up with her daughters in a closely besieged castle, he resolved to make an effort for their relief.

72

Accompanied by a troop which partook of
the gallantry of their commander, numbering
one hundred and twenty men, he set out,
probably from Oxford, and marching with a
degree of rapidity which anticipated all
intelligence of his design, he passed through
the quarters of Colonel Cook undiscovered,
and came to Wareham. The scarfs of Fairfax
had replaced their own; the sentinels saluted
the officer as he passed; and he rode with his
troop into the town, and directly up to the
governor's house. The governor aware that no
such troop was expected, took the alarm and
barricaded his lodgings, firing from thence
upon his assailants.

They had not much time to bestow on this
attack; therefore, in order to bring the contest
to a conclusion they set fire to a house in the
vicinity, which stood near to the powder
magazine, and the governor finding it
necessary to avoid this new danger, consented
to yield himself a prisoner, and was carried,
together with two committee-men mounted
behind some of the triumphant troopers, to
the foot of Corfe Castle.

Here a large force was drawn out to oppose
their further progress; but the gallant bearing
of this little troop, and the besieged shouting
their welcome from the walls prepared to
sally forth if a contest should commence,
induced the besiegers to give way. The gallant
band accomplished their purpose; and, whilst
tendering their services to the lady, they
presented also for her acceptance the prisoners
they had so gallantly captured.

The object of this chivalrous action was
probably an offer of escape to the ladies from
the castle; it was not, however, accepted, and
in their turn these brave men, surrounded by

73

superior forces, and not acquainted with the country, sustained a defeat from Colonel Cooke. Young Cromwell and some of his troopers, were taken prisoners, others of the troop escaped in various directions, and a portion of them, returning, found a refuge within the castle walls.

The course of events shifted rapidly now, and, though the lady of the castle was still as intrepid as at first, it was not so with all who were around her. The captive Governor of Wareham prevailed on Colonel Lawrence, hitherto so trustworthy, and still thought to be so, not only to connive at his escape, but to accompany him in his flight.

Final betrayal and destruction of Castle Spring 1646

And there was, within the walls, another traitor whose conduct was still more base, and his treachery far more fatal in its consequences.

Lt.-Colonel Pitman, an officer in the garrison, had served under the Earl of Inchequin in Ireland, and being weary of the king's service, let the enemy know that if he might have a protection, he would deliver the place to Parliament, which offer was accepted, transmitted to London, and a protection sent down.

On this he proposed to Colonel Anketil, the governor, that he would fetch one hundred men out of Somersetshire to reinforce the garrison, and would get leave of the enemy's commander, under pretence of procuring an exchange for his brother, then prisoner in the Parliament quarters, for one of the enemy's officers, who was prisoner in the castle.

This being approved of, he formed a design with Colonel Bingham, who commanded the siege, that under this colour he should convey above one hundred men into the castle, and as soon as they were entered the besiegers

74

should make an attack. On this, one hundred men were drawn out of Weymouth garrison, who marched to Lulworth Castle, where they were joined by thirty or forty more. **Treachery at work**

Pitman led them in the night to the post agreed upon for their entrance, where Colonel Anketil was ready to receive them. Some of them were in disguise, and knew every part of the castle. When 50 were entered the governor, seeing more behind, ordered the port to be shut, saying there were as many as he could dispose of.

Pitman expostulated with him for using him so ill, by causing him to bring men so far with the hazard of their lives, and expose them to the cold and the enemy. Those who entered possessed themselves of the king's and queen's towers, and the two platforms, expecting the time when the besiegers would make an assault, it being then two hours after midnight.

The besieged, as soon as the fraud was discovered, fired and threw down stones upon these intruders, but they maintained their post. There were in fact only six men of the garrison in the upper part of the castle, for that was considered impregnable. The remainder of the defending force was placed in the lower wards, which had been hitherto the posts of danger. The besieging forces, as soon as they saw their friends on the towers and platforms, began to advance; and it was then clear to the inmates of the castle that they were betrayed.

A parley was demanded, and the circumstance of a Parliamentary officer being there with the others of that party prisoners in the castle, induced the besiegers to offer conditions which were accepted.

But the truce was broken almost as soon as

it was agreed upon; two of the besiegers, anxious for the spoil, came over the wall by means of a ladder, some of the garrison fired upon them, and the risk now became imminent of a general slaughter throughout the castle.

Colonel Bingham, however, who was no hireling officer, but a descendant of a family long known and highly respected in the county, could not but admire the courage of the lady who was his foe, and he succeeded in preserving the lives of one hundred and forty persons then within the castle. Two of the garrison were killed, and one of the besiegers, in this final struggle. Thirty prisoners of the Parliamentary party being found in the castle were now set at liberty.

This last siege is said to have lasted forty-eight days, during which eleven men were slain and five ordnance taken. The day on which this catastrophe occurred is uncertain. No two of the writers living near the time agree in this respect. It occurred probably in the last week of the month of February.

By about the 7th April all the west country was cleared except Pendennis Castle and the siege of Oxford was expected.

The king now wrote to one of the few friends yet left to him, the Marquis of Ormond, informing him of his desperate condition, and of the resolution which he had consequently taken of throwing himself into the protection of the Scottish army, which was then engaged with the siege of Newark. On 27th April the king went out of Oxford, disguised, in the night time, two persons only accompanying him: Mr. John Ashburnham, a groom of his bed-chamber; and Mr. Hudson, a divine, his guide. On 5th May the king put himself in the power of the Scottish army, and with his sanction the city of Oxford surrendered to the Roundheads on the 24th of June.

A.D. 1646
5th May
The king
surrendered
to the
Scottish
Army

Thus, after a resistance of nearly three years duration this brave lady was dispossessed of the fortress which she continued to defend so long as a chance remained for the preservation of the crown, and when thus suddenly sent forth with her children to search for a home, it was her comfort to remember how faithful had been the attachment of all her humble neighbours, when the treachery of hireling strangers had accomplished what threats and force had failed to effect.

The work of plunder throughout the castle was soon achieved. Here were found stores of victuals and supplies, including seventeen barrels of powder, with match, etc. There are not a few of the fair mansions in Dorsetshire which have been constructed in a large measure with the stone and timber carried away from this castle.

The halls, galleries, and other chambers throughout the building were nobly decorated with rich tapestry and carpeting: other articles of furniture also, suitable in taste and value, which had remained probably since the splendid days of Sir Christopher Hatton, were there in abundance, and all of these fell into the hands of the despoilers.

The county sequestrators and officers commanding at the siege had been ordered by the Parliament to slight the castle, but the solidity of the walls defied in many parts even the force of gunpowder. Whole months were occupied in the endeavour, and heavy charges

A.D. 1646
House of
Commons
ordered
demolition
of Corfe
Castle

thrown upon the county rate for effecting the slow progress of this destruction, and in spite of all these endeavours, the remains of the castle present at this day one of the most imposing masses of architectural structure that are to be seen throughout the kingdom. These ruins have now ivy mantles on their towers, and the grass grows in the vaults and dungeons, but the lapse of centuries has had no more effect than the ravaging attempts of man, for destroying the substantial portions of the building.

One large tower was displaced many years ago by the effects of a violent storm and it rolled into the stream below. The weight of this mass is said to have shaken the ground to a degree which produced the effect of an earthquake throughout the neighbouring borough.

The triumphant Puritans, saw, in the heroic action of the lady a very just occasion for the forfeiture of her jointure.

The Dorsetshire Committee of Sequestration thus communicated to their superiors in London (quote from letters dated 4th June, 1646, Shaston):

> Since his decease she hath petitioned us to enjoy the jointure (estate) settled on her before the delinquency of her husband: but wee, fynding her active in the defence of Corfe Castle against the Parlyan[t] during her coverture, have not granted her desire, but conceive wee ought to continue the sequestration untill wee shall receive satisfaction from your Lordships whether her act during coverture includes her within the

ordinance, or whether your
Lordships bee not informed of any
delinquency in her since her
husband's decease, ffrom which
tyme the greatest part of her
residence hath been near London,
as wee are informed.

In the prosecution of this
sequestration wee shall be wholly
guided by your Lordships' advice.

Among Lady Bankes' papers were found
original copies of a publication named the
Dod, or Parliamentary Companion of the day.
It was divided into centuries, that is to say,
lists each containing a hundred names,
intended to be continued until it should
embrace the whole number of the House of
Commons. Two of these only were found
amongst Lady Bankes' papers. They were of
course much valued by the suffering families,
who could not but have had some curiosity to
know what had become of their forfeited
estates.

The list reads as follows:

"A list of the Names of the Members of the
House of Commons, observing which are
officers of the army, contrary to the Selfe-
denying Ordinance, together with such sums
of money, offices, and lands, as they have
given to themselves for service done and to
be done against the King and Kingdome.

The First Centurie"

and then it continues with the list of names.
A random example, taken from this list reads:

93. Sir William Purseby, Colonel and
Governor of Coventry, fought resolutely
against the Crosse in the Market-place at

79

Warwick, and against the antient monuments in the Earl's chappel in Saint Marie's church there, for which he had 1500£ given him; but when he should have fought with the enemie hid himself in the barley-field, for which a waterman at Temple staires (that had been his souldier) refused to carrie him."
and then, continuing:

"Besides the offices, commands, and gratuities, every member of the House of Commons, being in all 516, are by their own order allowed 4 pound per week a-man.

"By the Ordinance for sequestring delinquents (1 April 1643) it was declared that their estates should go for maintenance of the public affaires, and several ordinances designed Bishops' lands for to pay 200,000£ publique debt; yet by this and the following centuries thou shalt see how both delinquents' estates and Bishops' lands are by members of Parliament shared amongst themselves, whilst the 200,000£ is unpaid, the publique affaires supported by unsupportable taxes, and that Dutch divill, excise, that insensibly devoures the poore, and will impoverish the rich.

"These are they that breake the wooden yoke from our neckes and put on one of iron. Free us from a little ship-money paid thrice in an age, and impose as much at once for a monthly tax; quit us of the monopolies of tobacco, and set up excise on bread and beer. The first easeth the wanton rich man, and the latter grindeth the needy and poor."

Commonwealth declared May 19th 1649

Restoration of equity and justice   With Cromwell's accession to power the respect for equity and justice was in some measure restored, and Cromwell's judicial

80

appointments were in general above all exception.

The widowed heroine of the castle was no longer persecuted for her bravery; the attachment which bound Cromwell with warm affection to his daughters gave him a charitable disposition towards all who were of their sex. Large compensations being paid for herself and her children, Lady Bankes was now permitted to receive the annual amount of her jointure, and although claims upon her were from time to time brought forward in legal tribunals, of which records remain, she was not in any serious degree molested during the remainder of the period of the Commonwealth. She lived long enough to see the restoration of the monarchy, but died within a year thereafter.

The record of her death is thus inscribed on a monument of white marble in the chancel on the south side of the ancient church at Ruislip:

Arrangements made to assist Lady Mary Bankes

SIR RALPH BANKES.

TO THE MEMORY OF
THE LADY MARY BANKES ONELY
DAUGHTER OF RALPH HAWTREY OF RISLIPP
IN THE COUNTY OF MIDDX. ESQUIR
THE WIFE AND WIDOW OF THE HONble Sr
JOHN BANKES KNIGHT LATE LORD CHEIFE
JUSTICE OF HIS LATE MAJESTY'S COURT OF
COMMON PLEAS, AND OF THE PRIVY COUNCELL
TO HIS LATE MAJESTY KING CHARLES THE FIRST
OF BLESSED MEMORY
WHO HAVING HAD THE HONOR TO HAVE BORNE WITH
A CONSTANCY AND COURAGE ABOVE HER SEX A
NOBLE PROPORCION OF THE LATE CALAMATIES, AND
THE HAPPINESS TO HAVE OUTLIVED THEM SO FAR
AS TO HAVE SEENE THE RESTITUTION OF THE
GOVERNMENT WITH GREAT PEACE OF MIND
LAID DOWN HER MOST DESIRED LIFE, THE 11th DAY
OF APRIL 1661.

SIR RALPH HER SONNE AND HEIRE HATH
DEDICATED THIS.

Lady Bankes, brave to the last, with true Christian piety and courage faced death as she had confronted danger, careful to communicate neither pain nor apprehension to any one she loved. She gave to her relations so little expectation of her death, that her eldest son, then absent from her, being in Dorsetshire, was married on the morning of the day on which she died.

Sir Ralph Bankes was united to the descendant and heiress of the old Western family of the Brunes of Athelhampton and Plumber in Dorset. He had received the honour of knighthood from the new king. This, and some addition to the crest upon his coat of arms, were the recognitions of the loyal services of his house.

Sir Ralph was also permitted to recover the estates forfeited by his delinquent father if he could; and as it happened that they had not been specifically granted to any one of the 516 patriots who formed the Parliament of 1646, he had now the law on his side; whilst many persons similarly situated in point of suffering, were not equally fortunate in obtaining redress.

Restoration of Monarchy 1660, Charles II

In August 1660 was passed the celebrated Act for the settlement and quieting of the kingdom, called the Act of Indemnity and Oblivion, which the wits of that day interpreted by saying that "it was an act of indemnity for King Charles's enemies, and of oblivion for his friends".

The electors of Corfe Castle had chosen Sir Ralph Bankes for their representative in the

Parliament of Richard Cromwell, elected in 1658, and in 1660 Sir Ralph was re-elected by the same constituents for the Parliament of Charles II.

Taking his place now in the county to which he belonged as a person of some consideration, he had to provide himself with a habitation. The castle, which he had lost, no private fortune could have restored. It may be observed, also, that the feudal dignity and seclusion of the baronial age were by no means appreciated amongst the cavaliers of Charles II's day! Sir Ralph, however, had no desire to shine as a courtier, wisely preferring the honourable station to which he was born of a country gentleman. Fixing on a portion of his property he erected a mansion within the grounds which had formerly contained a residence of the Dukes of Somerset. There never was a period more favourable for the exercise of taste, as well in buildings as in decoration than this.

The house built by Sir Ralph Bankes was from a design of Inigo Jones, and the interior was decorated with portraits previously obtained from the pencil of Van Dyck, to which were now added many others executed by the great master Sir Peter Lely.

Whilst this building was in progress, Sir Ralph rented a place some few miles distant. Desirous of procuring solid materials for its construction, and also wishing to make provision of suitable articles of furniture to supply the apartments, he took active steps for tracing out the present possessors of the plunder of Corfe Castle. These included such articles as:

> Turkey and Persian carpets.
>
> A trunke, with all sorts of fine

The house built by Sir Ralph

Thought to be from designs left by Inigo Jones

A.D. 1660 April Building of Kingston Lacy commenced

Impression of Kingston Lacy (Pratt's design) in early days mid 1600's

In 1928 However detailed notes and sketches left by Sir Roger Pratt proved he designed it, and supervised building operations

child-bed linen, as sheets and pillow
cases and mantles.

A large suit of crimson velvet
chairs, stooles, couch embroydered,
long cushions of crimson velvet.

Many books and papers, at ye
value of 1300£, and new and good.

Furnitures for beds, purple, and
another crimson.

But from the records it would seem that
Sir Ralph recovered little from the hands of
the sequestrators, whom the law of the new
reign had indemnified—those items were: one
large bed, minus the feathers, and one red
velvet chair.

He completed his new mansion at Kingston
Lacy, and died when his son was under age.
He did not live to witness another revolution,
or to see the final expulsion of the Stuart
dynasty from the throne—that royal race, in
whose cause his family had suffered so
severely.

Impression of Kingston Lacy
after alterations by Sir Charles Barry, mid 1800's

HISTORICAL NOTES

HENRY OF ANJOU

On his second attempt to regain the throne, the eighteen-year-old Henry of Anjou (now Duke of Normandy and Acquitaine)], gained the support of many powerful followers. His military offensive pushed northwards from Bristol to the Midlands and back to Wallingford. Eventually he reached a firm agreement: Stephen would retain the throne until his death, but Henry would be recognised as his lawful heir. Henry II crowned 1154.

WAR OF THE ROSES (1455-1487)

This conflict lasted for a period of thirty years, during which time the House of Lancaster (Red Rose), and the House of York (White Rose) constantly tried to claim victory, to enable their House to provide England's King. During the course of the conflict almost all the great Nobles were killed, some in battle, some were executed as the battles were fought and victory swayed from one side to the other. Eventually, in the reign of Henry VII (1485-1509) the two Houses were at last united. An old couplet reminds us:
"With this seventh Henry
Both roses unite,
His own was the red
And his wife's was the white."

SIR JOHN BANKES

A good man and true. A Royalist. An intimate friend of Strafford. Maintained friendship on both sides during the Civil War. Was respected on both sides.

Descended from a good family seated in Keswick, Cumberland, where he was born. At Grammar School in the County. 1604 Queen's College, Oxford. No Degree. Took Chambers in Gray's Inn and applied himself to the Law. Lent-Reader at Gray's Inn, 1630, and in 1631 Treasurer of that Society. 1634 Knighted. Made Attorney General. 1640 Chief Justice of Common Pleas, made Lord Keeper. 1642 created Doctor of Laws at Oxford. Member of Privy Council. Died 28 December 1644. Interred in the Chapel of Christchurch, Oxford.

LADY MARY BANKES (died 11th April 1661)

Both prudent and courageous. Defended the castle against all assaults of the Roundheads. Closed gates of castle May 1643. Siege lifted 4th August 1643. Sir John after a short visit to his home and family returned to his duties in Oxford where Parliament reassembled in January 1644. Once again she put the castle in a state of defence. During the winter of 1644-45 she again held out. During this time Sir John died at Oxford in December 1644. She held out through 1645, although before the end of that year the king's cause was desperate. Finally the castle was surrended on 27th February 1646. On 5th March 1646 a vote was passed in House of Commons to demolish it.

CHARLES I (Born 1600. Aceded 1625. Beheaded 1649)

Charles I succeeded his father James I as King in 1625. He believed being King entitled him to be above the Law.

The King was soon in conflict with Parliament. The people were complaining bitterly of unfair taxation. They rebelled also because his was a personal rule, and not rule by Law. A particularly unpopular Tax was introduced at this time – a Levy which became known as 'Ship Money' – to provide ships for the Navy. It caused particular resentment in inland counties and its revival by Charles I played a vital part in the outbreak of the Civil War.

In 1628 Parliament presented a declaration to the King, calling it *THE PETITION OF RIGHT*. Among other things it demanded that it should be unlawful for the King to impose taxes without the consent of Parliament; that people should not be imprisoned unless they were first brought to trial and proved to have broken the Law.

The Petition was signed by the King but he broke his promises almost at once.

In 1641 because of the King's broken promises Parliament accused him of talking away the liberties of the people, and in August 1642 the Civil War finally started. On 4th June 1647 the King surrendered to Parliament and he was arrested. His trial took place in Westminster Hall in London. There he was tried and condemned to death. He was beheaded in front of Banqueting House, Whitehall, on 30 January 1649. The Commonwealth was declared on 19th May, 1649.

CHARLES II (Born 1630. Acceded 1660. Died 1685)

During the Civil War Charles II was in command of the royalist forces in the west. The final battle on 14th June, at Naseby, brought victory for Cromwell and defeat for Charles who escaped to the Continent.

After the death of Cromwell in 1658, a short rule of Protector Richard Cromwell (1658-59). Then Cromwell's trusted General Monck took the lead in bringing back Charles II from the continent to rule in England. He was made king in 1660. During the early years of his reign he was popular with the people who were now by now rather weary of the sober times following the death of Charles I.

As time went on he became more selfish, and wildly extravagant, forgetting those who had served him well; in particular Edward Hyde, Earl of Clarendon, his chief adviser, who had been faithful to him in exile.

OLIVER CROMWELL

After the death of Charles I. Cromwell, strongly backed by the Army and Parliament, was installed as head of the Commonwealth. He was Lord Protector from 1653 to his death.

Originally a farmer in Huntingdonshire, he was a brave and religious man. He was opposed to the King. His followers dressed in sober clothes – a complete contrast to the extravagance of the Court. He was willing to come forward as a champion of rights of the people in his own part of the country. He gathered increasing power and support. He became a Member of Parliament where he soon made a name for himself because of his enthusiasm for the popular cause. In the early days his uncouth manners and rough speech offended many, but his earnestness gained him respect.

In 1641 because of the King's broken promises Parliament accused him of talking away the liberties of the people, and in August 1642 the Civil War finally started. On 4th June 1647 the King surrended to Parliament and he was arrested. His trial took place in Westminster Hall in London. There he was tried and condemned to death. He was beheaded in front of Banqueting House, Whitehall, on 30 January 1649. The Commonwealth was decleared on 19th May, 1649.

TIME AND TIDE

Candle Clock: Reference to historians of Alfred's time provides us with differing accounts of the measurement of time and means of artificial light.

Spelman tells us that Alfred measured time by means of wax candles marked by "circular lines of divers colours". These were tended by the "keepers of his chapel, whose office it was to put him in mind how each hour passed".

Asser records that he used candles as timekeepers to divide his working day. It is likely that he used them as "interval timers". Each candle burned away in four hours and was enclosed in a lantern made of wood with horn windows to keep out of the draughts.

The horn used in the making of lanterns was scraped until very, very thin. Glass at this time was hardly known. Though a draught excluder the light given by the candle must have been correspondingly diminished by the use of the horn.

Tide: Eric Burton in his *Dictionary of Clocks and Watches,* records that the Saxons divided a day into eight tides of three hours each, shown by their *sundials.* These tides were:

MORGAN	4.30 a.m.– 7.30 a.m.
DAEG-MAEL	7.30 a.m.–10.30 a.m.
MID-DAG	10.30 a.m.– 1.30 p.m.
AFANVERTH DAGR	1.30 p.m.– 4.30 p.m.
MID-AFTEN	4.30 p.m.– 7.30 p.m.
ONDVERTH NOTT	7.30 p.m.–10.30 p.m.
MID-NIHT	10.30 p.m.– 1.30 a.m.

Wax Tapers: These were used also. Obviously much more dangerous as a fire risk.

Wax: probably beeswax. *Tallow:* from animal fat. Both probably used.

ENGLISH MONARCHS

SAXONS	Began to reign	Reigned	Died
Alfred the Great	871		
Edward the Elder	901		
Athelstan	925		
Edmund the Magnificent	940		
Edred	946		
Edwy	955		
Edgar the Peaceable	958		
Edward the Martyr	975		
Ethelred II (The Unready)	979-1013	Retired on Sweyn's Proclamation restored in Canute's absence on Sweyn's death	
	1014-1016		
Edmund II (Ironside)	1016	Divided the kingdom with Canute for seven months	
DANES			
Sweyn	1013-1014		
Canute	1017-1035		
Harold I	1035-1040		
Hardicanute	1040-1042		
SAXONS RESTORED			
Edward the Confessor	1042-1066		
Harold II	1066		
NORMAN CONQUEST ONWARDS			
William I	1066	21 years	1087
William II	1087	13 ,,	1100
Henry I	1100	35 ,,	1135
Stephen	1135	19 ,,	1154
PLANTAGENETS			
Henry II	1154	35 ,,	1189
Richard I	1189	10 ,,	1199
John	1199	17 ,,	1216
Henry III	1216	56 ,,	1272
Edward I	1272	35 ,,	1307
Edward II	1307	20 ,,	1327
Edward III	1327	50 ,,	1377
Richard II	1377 (deposed 1399)	22 ,,	
House of Lancaster			
Henry IV	1399	13 ,,	1413
Henry V	1413	9 ,,	1422
Henry VI	1422 (deposed 1461)	39 ,,	

	Began to reign		Reigned		Died
House of York					
Edward IV	1461		22	,,	1483
Edward V	1483				1483
Richard III	1483		2	,,	1485
TUDORS					
Henry VII	1485		24	years	1509
Henry VIII	1509		38	,,	1547
Edward VI	1547		6	,,	1553
Mary I	1553		5	,,	1558
Elizabeth I	1558		44	,,	1603
STUARTS					
James I (VI of Scotland)	1603		22	,,	1625
Charles I	1625		24	,,	1649 (Beheaded)
Commonwealth					
declared 19th May	1649				
Oliver Cromwell					
Lord Protector	1653-1658				
Richard Cromwell	1658-1659				
Charles II	1660		25	,,	1685
James II	1685	Abdicated 1688	3	,,	1701 (in exile)
William III and Mary II	1689				
Anne	1702		12	,,	1714
HOUSE OF HANOVER					
George I	1714		13	,,	1727
George II	1727		33	,,	1760
George III	1760		59	,,	1820
George IV	1820		10	,,	1830
William IV	1830		7	,,	1837
Victoria	1837		63	,,	1901
HOUSE OF SAXE-COBURG-GOTHA					
Edward VII	1901		9	,,	1910
HOUSE OF WINDSOR					
George V	1910		25	,,	1936
Edward VIII	1936	Abdicated	326	days	
George VI	1936		15	years	1952
Elizabeth II	1952